IMAGES OF WAR
THE RED BARON

Dedication

This book is dedicated to my good friend Clive Ponsford, who introduced me to flying 'string bag' biplanes during our college days, and has kept whetting my appetite later in life with frequent sorties in his beautifully restored Tiger Moth.

IMAGES OF WAR
THE RED BARON

RARE PHOTOGRAPHS FROM WARTIME ARCHIVES

BARRY PICKTHALL

Pen & Sword
MILITARY

First published in Great Britain in 2016 by
PEN & SWORD MILITARY
an imprint of
Pen & Sword Books Ltd,
47 Church Street, Barnsley,
South Yorkshire.
S70 2AS

ISBN 978-1-47383-358-6

A CIP catalogue record for this book is available
from the British Library

Typeset by Mac Style Ltd, Bridlington, East Yorkshire
Printed and bound in Great Britain by CPI

Pen & Sword Books Ltd incorporates the imprints of
Pen & Sword Aviation, Pen & Sword Family History, Pen & Sword Maritime,
Pen & Sword Military, Pen & Sword Discovery, Wharncliffe Local History,
Wharncliffe True Crime, Wharncliffe Transport, Pen and Sword Select,
Pen and Sword Military Classics

For a complete list of Pen & Sword titles please contact:
PEN & SWORD BOOKS LIMITED
47 Church Street, Barnsley, South Yorkshire, S70 2AS, England.
E-mail: enquiries@pen-and-sword.co.uk
Website: www.pen-and-sword.co.uk

Contents

Introduction

This story began, not above the bloody trenches of the Somme during World War I, but a century later with the discovery of a 'lost' archive of black and white negatives bought as a job lot from a car boot sale in Sussex. As the owner of a picture library, I am always on the lookout for historic images to swell our 'PPL Pictures of Yesteryear' archive. What first caught my eye were some old black and white prints of Sussex scenes stacked in a shoebox. Hidden beneath was an envelope stuffed full of negatives and badly degraded contact prints. I bought the lot for £20 and it was not until some months later when we began to look at the collection of old planes under a magnifying glass, that we realised the magnitude of this find.

The first clue was the German markings; the second was of a dashing young man who appeared in the majority of the pictures. It did not take long to recognise him as the First World War German fighter ace Baron Manfred von Richthofen.

The next question: How did this remarkable collection finish up in a car boot sale? We may never know the definitive answer to that, but almost certainly, the archive of negatives, which include rare pictures of British, French and German planes, together with images of other air aces from both sides, had come from a house clearance where the pictures had been stored away for many years. Clearly, someone with a keen interest in The Red Baron had pulled this collection

2nd Lieutenant Lionel Morris, Baron Von Richthofen's first victim in aerial combat. Lionel was 19 when killed, and was one of two Whitgift School 'old boys' to feature in the Red Baron's life story.

Major General George W Barber, the Australian doctor who performed an autopsy on Baron Von Richthofen's body and found that he had been killed by a single .303 bullet fired from the ground, most probably shot by Australian forces, and not by Canadian pilot Captain Arthur 'Roy' Brown who is still commonly credited with shooting down the Red Baron. George Barber was the second Whitgift School 'old boy' to become associated with Manfred Von Richthofen's life.

together for it also includes images of the German's greatest rivals including Major Lanoe George Hawker VC, DSO, American Captain Edward Vernon Rickenbacker and Frenchman Georges Marie Ludovic Jules Guynemer. Subsequent research shows that while some of the images had not been published before, others have. One historian has suggested that during and after the War, official photographers made copy negatives of some prints for distribution to those involved in the pictures and it is these negatives that make up this collection.

Our own efforts to identify each image led us down many paths, but the most remarkable one was to discover a less familiar autobiography published in 1918 after Richthofen's death and cessation of hostilities. This work provides a valuable insight into what motivated this pilot to become the 'Top Gun' of his era.

Perhaps our anonymous collector of Red Baron pictures was also planning to publish? If so, then this book combines two forgotten dreams.

There is one more coincidental twist to this story about the rise and fall of Manfred von Richthofen – the part played by two 'old boys' from Whitgift School, Croydon. Second Lieutenant Lionel Bertram Frank Morris had left the school in 1915 to become an articled clerk with a firm of solicitors working in the heart of London's legal district. He got his pilot's certificate early in 1916 and became the Red Baron's first victim. Morris was just 19.

Lieutenant Colonel George Walter Barber was much older and survived the War. He too was a Whitgift 'old boy' who became a doctor and emigrated to Western Australia in 1895. He served in the Somme and performed the autopsy on von Richthofen's body that determined that the German flying ace had been killed by a single .303 rifle bullet fired from the ground, rather than the still popular myth that he had been shot down by Canadian Captain Arthur 'Roy' Brown.

Historical note
Prior to October 1916 Germany's air force (excluding German naval aviation) was called the *Fliegertruppen des Deutschen Kaiserreiches* (Imperial German Flying Corps). Thereafter it became the *Deutsche Luftstreitkrafte* (German Air Force). Whichever force was extent, both were part of Germany's army.

German force and unit names do not always translate readily into an equivalent English language name or formation. Consequently, to most Britons (then and since), Germany's air forces throughout World War I were commonly, and erroneously, referred to as the Imperial German Air Service.

Barry Pickthall
February 2016

Acknowledgements
Special credit must be given to the von Richthofen Archive/PPL (www.pplmedia.com) and also to Martin Derry, the editor of this project, who provided additional images and guided the project towards completion.

Chapter One

Formative Years

As his title suggests, Baron Manfred von Richthofen was born to privilege. His ancestors had vast estates in the Breslau and Striegau regions of Germany, and the few who did not inherit their wealth, entered government service.

Born on 2 May 1892, Manfred's mother was from the von Schickfuss line of landed gentry, which had more experience of war. Her great uncle had fallen in 1806, and during the revolution of 1848, the family home, one of the finest castles in Schickfuss, had been ransacked and burnt.

For both families, the principle focus was keeping their estates and the pleasures of horse riding, hunting and shooting. Manfred was named after his uncle, who in peace time, was adjutant to the German emperor Wilhelm II, and commander of the Corps of Cavalry. His father was also a professional soldier who had entered the cadet corps as a boy and later enlisted as a cavalry officer with the 12th Regiment of Uhlans. His claim to fame was to rescue one of his men from drowning during a winter exercise. Wet through, he then insisted on continuing as if nothing had happened, taking no notice of the weather. As a result, he caught an ear infection that led to partial deafness, a disability that forced him to leave the service.

Circa 1917: Portrait of Germany's fighter ace Baron Manfred von Richthofen who ultimately was credited with 80 victories – the greatest number secured by any pilot on either side during the First World War.

The young Manfred was tutored privately until his ninth birthday when he went to school for a year in Schweidnitz before joining the cadet corps in Wahlstatt, prior to following in his father's footsteps by entering the 1st Regiment of Uhlans. By all accounts, this was not his choice of career, and not an enjoyable time. He wrote:

Circa 1915: Frieda von Richthofen, mother of Baron Manfred von Richthofen.

'I was not particularly eager to become a Cadet, but my father wished it, so my wishes were not consulted. I found the strict discipline difficult to bear and did not care much for the instruction I received. I never was good at learning things and did just enough work to pass. In my opinion it would have been wrong to do more than was just sufficient, and as a consequence, my teachers did not think overmuch of me.

On the other hand, I was very fond of sport, particularly gymnastics, football and other outdoor activities. I could do all kinds of tricks on the horizontal bar and received various prizes from the Commander.

I had a tremendous liking for risky foolery. For instance, my friend Frankenberg and I climbed the famous steeple of Wahlstatt by means of the lightning conductor and tied a handkerchief to the top. Ten years on I was intrigued to see my handkerchief was still tied to the top of the spire when I visited my younger brother when he was a Cadet, and remember just how difficult it was to negotiate the gutters.'

Von Richthofen much preferred his time at the Lichterfelde War Academy.

'I did not feel so isolated from the world and began to live a little more like a human being. My happiest reminiscences from Lichterfelde are sporting ones against my great opponent Prince Frederick Charles. The Prince gained many first prizes against me both in running and football, because I had not trained nearly as well as he.'

It was a lesson well learned that was to serve him in good stead later. Manfred joined the 1st Regiment of *Uhlans* over Easter in 1911 and graduated from the War Academy in the autumn of 1912

'It was a glorious feeling being given my epaulettes. People started to call me 'Lieutenant'. It was the finest I have ever experienced.'

His Father presented him with a horse named Santuzza as a graduation present. The mare was a marvellous specimen, as hard as nails, which could keep her place in a procession yet when required, also jump incredible heights. Manfred set out to train her, but during a final ride before both were to be put on a train to their first posting, the horse slipped in the training ground while jumping a fence, tossing Van Richthofen off in the process. Manfred broke his collarbone and Santuzza damaged a shoulder, which spelled the end of their partnership.

But this was not the end of his sporting exploits in the saddle, nor falls from grace:

'Another time, I had the good fortune to ride a very fine horse at a horse show in Breslau. My horse did extremely well and I had hopes of succeeding. Approaching the last obstacle, I saw from a distance a great crowd watching around it and realised that it was bound to be something extraordinary. I thought to myself: "Keep your spirits up. You are sure to get into trouble!"

I made our approach at full speed, neither seeing nor hearing the crowd waving and shouting not to go so fast. My horse jumped, and only as we straddled the jump did we see the steep slope down to the River Weistritz. In one a gigantic leap we landed in the river, and both horse and rider disappeared. I was thrown over the head of the animal and finally got out of the water on the opposite side to where Felix my horse had been attracted. When I came back to be weighed in, the stewards were surprised that I had put on 10 pounds instead of losing the usual 2. No one noticed that I was wet through.'

Von Richthofen had more success with his charger named *Blume*:

'He was very good, having learned to do everything: running, steeplechasing, jumping, army service. There was nothing it had not learned and I enjoyed several successes with him. One of these was when competing for the Kaiser Prize in 1913. I was the only one to get a clear round, but in doing so, had an experience, which could not easily be repeated. The course took in a piece of heathland, and at full gallop I suddenly found myself standing on my head. The horse had stepped into a rabbit hole, and the fall left me with a broken collarbone. I remounted and rode on without making a mistake and finished in good time.'

War clouds gather

The First World War led to the slaughter of 17 million people, traumatised a generation, overturned old empires and changed the world's political order forever. It was triggered by the assassination of Franz Ferdinand, the Archduke of Austria-Hungary on June 28, 1914. It was his death at the hands of Gavrilo Princip – a Serbian nationalist with ties to the secretive military group known as *The Black Hand* that propelled the major European military powers into open conflict

It began with Austria-Hungary declaring war on Serbia, a month to the day after the Archduke's assassination, and was followed in short order by Germany declaring war on France and invading Belgium, which led Britain to declare war on Germany.

At the time, Europe was dominated by 6 major powers, which divided into two broad groups with Britain, France and Russia forming the *Triple Entente*, and Germany, Austria-Hungary and Italy joining forces as the *Triple Alliance*.

Yet the inevitability of war was lost on young cavalry officers like von Richthofen, who wrote in his autobiography:

'We had become accustomed to war talk and had been ordered to pack our service kit so often that the whole thing had become tedious. No one believed any longer that there would be war. We, were close to the border and were "the eyes of the Army", to use the words of my Commander, but no one believed there would be war.

On the day before military preparations began, we were sitting in the officers' club 10k from the border, eating oysters, drinking champagne and gambling a little. We were very merry. No one thought of war.

During a very decent luncheon we were disturbed by Count Kospoth, the Administrator of Ols, who looked like a ghost. We greeted our old friend with a loud Hoorah! He explained that he had come personally to the border to ascertain whether the rumours of an impending world-war were true, assumed, correctly, that the best information could only be obtained on the front.

He was surprised to say the least to see our peaceful assembly. We learned from him that all the bridges in Silesia were being patrolled by the military and that steps were being taken to fortify various positions. We convinced him that the possibility of war was absolutely nil and continued with our festivities.'

The next day, von Richthofen and his men were ordered to the Front.

To cavalrymen, the word 'war' was not unfamiliar. This after all is what they had trained for. But while everyone knew what to do and what to leave undone, no one within this troop had any idea what would happen next. All every soldier wanted was to be able to show their ability and value to the group.

Their orders were to study the ground, work towards the rear of the enemy, and to destroy important targets. Their problem was finding out where the enemy was:

'At Midnight, I rode at the head of a file of soldiers against the enemy for the first time with orders in my pocket. A river marked the border and I expected to be fired on when we reached it, but to my astonishment we passed over the bridge without an incident. The next morning, we reached the church tower of the village of Kieltze without seeing anything of the enemy or rather without being seen by him.

The question was what should I do in order not to be noticed by the villagers? My first idea was to lock up the priest. We fetched him from his house, and to his great surprise, locked him up among the bells in the church tower, took away the ladder and left him sitting up above. I assured him that he would be executed if the population should show any hostile inclinations. A sentinel placed on the tower observed the neighbourhood.'

Everything remained quiet for five nights. It was on the sixth that their peace was interrupted by the call from a lookout 'the Cossacks are here!' The night was pitch dark, it was raining and no stars were visible. Neither side could see more than a metre ahead of them.
Von Richthofen and his men had previously breached the wall around the churchyard as a precaution though which they now led their horses into the open. Working his way along the churchyard wall with his lookout, Manfred found the main street swarming with twenty to thirty Cossacks.

Most carried lanterns, and were incautiously loud. One left his horse and went to find the priest who had been released the day before. The thought flashed through his mind 'we are about to be betrayed!' and had to be doubly careful, I could not risk a fight because I could not fire more than two carbines, and resolved to play cops and robbers with them.

There was no need, for after resting a few hours, the Cossacks rode away again. It was von Richthofen who eventually got the biggest surprise. After returning to their garrison on the seventh day, he related:

'Everyone stared at me as if I were a ghost – not due to my unshaven face, but word that I had fallen at Kalisch. The place, the time and all the circumstances of my death had been reported in such detail that word had spread throughout Silesia. My mother had already received visits of condolence. The only thing that had been omitted was an announcement in the newspaper.'

To France
Von Richthofen received orders for him and his cavalrymen to take a train. No one knew where it was going. Their only instruction was to pack provisions for a long journey. Rumours flew around like startled starlings, but they were only that – rumours. Their one clue was that the train was facing westward. Manfred wrote:

'A second-class compartment had been given to four of us. But within a day we discovered that a second-class compartment is altogether too narrow for four warlike youths and we resolved to distribute ourselves better. I rearranged part of a luggage car, which had light, air and plenty of space, and converted it into a bedroom/drawing room. I found straw at one of the stations, put a tent cloth over the top and slept as well as I did in my four-poster bed in Ostrowo.

We travelled night and day, first through Silesia, and then Saxony, going westward all the time. We were heading in the direction of Metz but even the train conductor had no idea where we were going. At every station, even at those that we did not stop at, huge crowds feted us with cheers and flowers. We had been at war for only a week and it was already evident that the German nation was seized with wild enthusiasm. We Uhlans were admired in particular.

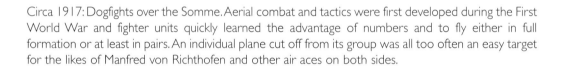

Circa 1917: Dogfights over the Somme. Aerial combat and tactics were first developed during the First World War and fighter units quickly learned the advantage of numbers and to fly either in full formation or at least in pairs. An individual plane cut off from its group was all too often an easy target for the likes of Manfred von Richthofen and other air aces on both sides.

Those who had passed through before us must have reported that we had met the enemy, and anyway, my regiment had been mentioned in the first official communiqué. The 1st Regiment of Uhlans and the 155th Regiment of Infantry had taken Kalisch. We were treated as heroes and naturally enough, we felt like heroes.

One of our number had found a Cossack sword, which he now showed to admiring girls, making a great impression with it. Of course, we asserted that blood was sticking to it and invented hair-raising tales. At one point we were held up in a long tunnel. It is uncomfortable enough to stop in a tunnel in peacetime, but to stop suddenly in war is much worse. Some excited, high-spirited fellow wanted to play a joke and fired a shot. Before long there was general firing in the tunnel. It was surprising that no one was hurt.

We remained very happy and wild until disembarking from the train at Busendorf, near Diedenhofen. The heat was so great that our horses almost collapsed.'

The following day, they marched northward towards Luxemburg and the first fortified towns of Belgium. No one knew what relations with the inhabitants of this little state would be like. When von Richthofen met a Luxemburg prisoner and was told he would complain to the Emperor about him if he was not freed immediately, Manfred saw no reason not to, and let him go.

To the left and to the right, before and behind them, troops were marching on every road, advancing just as they had been taught during manoeuvres. It suddenly struck Manfred that from all this disorder, a wonderfully arranged plan was evolving.

He also became aware of the flying corps for the first time.

'I was quite ignorant about the activities of our flying men, and got tremendously excited whenever I saw an aviator. Of course I had no idea whether it was a German airman, or the enemy, for we had no knowledge that the German machines were marked with crosses and the enemy machines with circles. As a consequence, we fired at every plane we saw!'

At Arlon, (situated on the borders of Luxemburg and Belgium) Manfred left his men outside the town and rode in alone by bicycle to climb the church steeple.

'Of course, I saw nothing of the enemy who were still far away, but when I came down, I was surrounded by a group of angry young men. The tyres on my bicycle had, of course, been let down, leaving me no option but to go back on foot. Had it come to a fight, I would have been delighted because, with a pistol in my hand, I felt absolutely sure of myself.

Later, I heard that the inhabitants had behaved very seditiously towards our cavalry and our hospital, and it had been necessary to place quite a number of these gentlemen against a wall. I also learned that my cousin had been killed close to the town, just three days before.'

Family tragedy apart, von Richthofen reflected fondly on those early days:

'We cavalrymen, those of us who had already engaged with the enemy and seen something of war, were envied by the men from other divisions who had not. For me, it was the most beautiful time during the whole of the war and I would much like to pass through those times again.'

The first bullets

Von Richthofen and his men were ordered to ascertain the strength of the enemy occupying a large forest near Virton in Belgium. Riding with fifteen *Uhlans*, he thought:

'Today I shall have my first fight with the enemy. It was a beautiful August morning and the forest seemed at peace until they picked up the traces left by a large number of cavalry horses that must have passed by shortly before.

It lies in the instinct of every German to rush at the enemy, particularly when meeting hostile cavalry. In my mind's eye I saw myself at the head of my little troop slashing through a hostile squadron with our sabres, and felt quite intoxicated by it all. As we followed the spoor at a rapid trot, the eyes of my Uhlans sparkled with joyful expectation.

After an hour-long ride, the wood became thinner, I felt convinced that here we would meet the enemy. To the right of our narrow path was a steep rocky wall many metres high and to the left, a narrow rivulet. Ahead was a meadow, 50 metres wide, surrounded by barbed wire. Suddenly, the trace of hooves disappeared into bushes across a bridge. My leading men stopped because our exit from the forest was blocked by a barricade.

There was movement among the bushes and immediately I realised that we had fallen into a trap. I then noticed dismounted cavalrymen with a hundred rifles or more pointed towards us. With the path ahead blocked, steep rocks to the right and barbed wire surrounding the meadow. Seconds later I heard the first shot followed by very intensive rifle fire from a distance of 50-100 metres. There was nothing to be done but go back, so I lifted my arm and beckoned my men to follow. Possibly, they misunderstood my gesture. Believing I was in danger, they charged down the narrow path towards me. The confusion and panic that followed was heightened tenfold by the noise of each shot. The last I saw of them was as they leaped the barricade, and never heard anything of them again. Doubtless they were made prisoners of war.

I turned my horse and gave him the spurs, probably for the first time during his life. I had the greatest difficulty to make the remaining Uhlans understand that they should turn round and get away. The enemy had surprised us completely. They had probably been watching us from the very beginning, and in typical French character, had planned to catch us unawares from the outset.

The horse that my orderly was riding at my side was hit and fell. Other horses were rolling all around me, and in the wild disorder I jumped over them. The last I saw of my orderly, he was lying under his horse, apparently not wounded, but pinned down by the weight of the animal.

Two days later, I was delighted when he turned up wearing only one boot, having left the other one under the body of his horse. At least two squadrons of French cuirassiers had jumped out of the forest and plundered the fallen horses and brave Uhlans. He had escaped by climbing the rocks and hiding in the bushes for two hours, before walking back to our base. He could tell me little about the fate of our comrades left behind.'

The battle of Virton

Von Richthofen and his men were tasked with tracking enemy movements. The French were in retreat and it took all day to reach their lines and despatch a report back to headquarters. The question then was whether to ride back through the night or rest up close to the enemy lines and set out refreshed the following morning. With the French on the back foot, he thought it safe enough to stay, and took his men to a monastery with large stables nearby.

'When we entered our new home, the enemy was so near that they could have shot us through the windows, but the monks were extremely amiable. They gave us as much to eat and to drink as we cared to have and we had a very good time. The saddles were taken off the horses – a dead weight of 150kgs – for the first time in three days and nights, which made them happy and we settled down as if we were in the house of a delightful host and friend. My friend Loen and I had quarters for ourselves, and having posted a guard, got into our nightshirts, jumped into bed, and let the Lord look after us.

In the middle of the night someone suddenly flung open the door and shouted: "Sir. The French are here!" I was too sleepy and too heavy to be able to reply. Loen, who was similarly incapacitated, gave the most intelligent answer: "How many are they?" The soldier stammered, full of excitement, "We have shot dead two, but we cannot say how many there are for it is pitch dark." I heard Loen reply in a sleepy tone: "All right. When more arrive, call me again." Half a minute later both of us were snoring again.

As it happened, the French had passed by our castle during the night and our guards had fired on them. Since it was a very dark night nothing further followed. When we woke up next morning, the sun was already high in the heavens. We took an ample breakfast and then continued our journey, but not before hanging several of our hosts from the lanterns because they could not overcome their desire to take a hand in the war.

Later, we rode over the battlefield that our Division had been fighting and found it to be occupied not by German soldiers, but French Red Cross men. They looked as surprised at seeing us as we did them. Nobody thought of shooting and as we cleared out, it dawned on us that instead of advancing, our troops, had retreated. Fortunately, the enemy were also on the retreat in the opposite direction, otherwise I would now be somewhere in captivity.

Late in the afternoon we reached our regiment quite satisfied with the course of events that had taken place during the previous 24 hours.'

Boredom before Verdun

Von Richthofen always described himself as a 'restless spirit', so the lack of activity at the Front during the build-up to the battle of Verdun he found tiresome to the extreme. Stationed some 1,500 metres behind the forward trenches in a bomb-proofed heated shelter, he lacked for nothing – other than action! He volunteered to become a despatch bearer in the hope of some adventures, but was treated as a worthless 'base-hog' by the fighting men.

'Now and then I had to go to the front trenches. That meant great physical exertion trudging uphill and down, criss-crossing, through an unending number of trenches and mire holes until at last one arrived at a place where men were firing. My position seemed to me, to be a very stupid one.

At that time, the business of digging was just beginning. I had learned the names of the various ditches and holes at the War Academy, but the digging itself was the task of military engineers. We were not supposed to take a hand in it. Here, near Combres, everyone was digging industriously. Each soldier had a spade and a pick and took great trouble to dig as deeply as possible. It was very strange that in many places the French were only five metres ahead of us. We could hear them speak and see them smoke cigarettes. Now and then they would threw us a piece of paper. We conversed with them, but tried to annoy them in every possible way, especially with hand grenades.

Around us, the once dense forest of the Cote Lorraine had been cut down by the vast number of shells and bullets, which were being fired unceasingly. It seemed unbelievable that men could survive such conditions. None the less, the men at the Front were to my mind, not in as bad a position as the men back at base. After a morning visit to the front trenches, which usually took place in the early hours of the day, the more tedious business began. I had to attend to the telephone.

On days when I was off duty, I indulged in my favourite pastime – game shooting. When going for a ride in the forest of La Chaussee I had noticed that wild boar were about and found out where I could shoot them at night. We had some beautiful nights, with a full moon and snow, and with the assistance of my orderly, I built a shelter seat in a tree at a spot where the pigs passed by. I spent many nights sitting on the branch of a tree and turned into an icicle the following morning before getting my reward.

There was a sow that swam across the lake and broke into a potato field, always at the same spot, and then swam back again. I was very keen to make my acquaintance with the animal, so made a seat on the far shore of the lake. Auntie Pig appeared for her supper at midnight and I shot her while she was still swimming and managed to seize her by the leg before she drowned.

Another time, I was riding with my orderly along a narrow path just as several wild boar were crossing it. I jumped from my horse, grasped my orderly's carbine and rushed several hundred metres ahead. At the end of the procession came a mighty boar. I had never seen such a beast and now its head hangs in my room as a reminder of these encounters.

Several months passed by in this manner until one day, our division became busy planning a small attack. I was delighted, for now at last I would be able to do something connected to the war. But it led to yet another disappointment – I was given quite a different job. I had enough, and in my frustration, sent a letter to my Commanding General saying: "My dear Excellency! I did not go to war simply to collect cheese and eggs, but for another purpose."

Initially, those above me simply snarled at me but then fulfilled my wish. Thus I joined the Flying Service.

Chapter Two

First Flight

Manfred von Richthofen was transferred to the Imperial German Air Service at the end of May 1915, saying:

'My greatest wish was fulfilled. At 7 o'clock I flew for the first time as an observer. I was very excited but had no idea what it would be like. Everyone I asked told me a different tale. The previous night, I had gone to bed earlier than usual in order to be thoroughly refreshed for when we drove over to the airfield the following morning, and got into a flying machine for the first time.

The draught from the propeller was a particular nuisance and I found it impossible to make myself understood. Everything was carried away by the wind. If I took up a piece of paper it disappeared. My safety helmet slid off. My muffler dropped off. My jacket was not buttoned sufficiently. In short, I felt very uncomfortable.

Before I knew it, the pilot went ahead at full speed and the machine started rolling. We went faster and faster. I clutched the sides of the cockpit. Suddenly, the shaking was over, the machine was in the air and the earth dropped away from under me.

It was my job to direct the pilot to the place we were to fly to. At first we flew right ahead but then my pilot turned first to the right, and then to the left, and soon I lost all sense of direction and had not the slightest notion of where we were! I cautiously looked over the side down at the country below. The men looked ridiculously small and the houses seemed to come out of a child's toy box. Everything seemed pretty. Cologne was in the background and the cathedral looked like a little toy.

Circa 1916: An autographed photograph of Baron Manfred von Richthofen, in the cockpit of an Albatros fighter.

To be so high above the earth and master of the air was a glorious feeling. I didn't care a bit where we were and was extremely disappointed when my pilot thought it was time to go down again. I would have liked nothing better than to set out on another flight immediately.

I have never had any trouble in the air such as vertigo. I find the celebrated American fairground rides to be very uncomfortable. One does not feel secure in them. But in a flying machine, there is a feeling of complete security. You sit in a plane just as you would in an easy chair. Vertigo is impossible. No man has been turned giddy by flying, but at the same time, flying does affect one's nerves. When one races full speed through the air, and particularly when descending down again, when the plane dips suddenly, the engine stops running, and when the tremendous noise is followed by an equally tremendous silence, then I would frantically clutch the sides and think we were sure to fall to the ground. But everything happened in such a matter-of-fact and natural way, and when we again touched terra firma, the landing was so simple. I was full of enthusiasm and would have liked nothing better than to remain in a plane all day long. I counted the hours to the time when we would start out again.'

Observing for Mackensen in Russia

'On the 10th of June 1915 I was sent to the Front. I was anxious to go forward as quickly as possible because I feared I might get there too late, that the war might be over. If I were to spend three months training to become a pilot, peace might have been concluded.

It never occurred to me to become a pilot. I imagined that my training as a cavalryman would serve me well as an observer. I was very happy that, after a fortnight's flying experience, I was sent out, especially since I was sent to the only spot where there was still a chance of action. I was sent to Russia.'

'Mackensen was advancing gloriously. He had broken through the Russian position at Gorlice and I joined his army when we were taking Rawa Ruska. I spent a day at the airfield before being sent to the celebrated 69th Squadron. Being quite a beginner, I felt very foolish. My pilot was a big gun. First Lieutenant Zeumer. He is now a cripple. Of the other men within the Section, I am the only survivor. This was my most beautiful time. Life in the Flying Corps is very much like life in the cavalry. Every day, morning and afternoon, I had to fly and reconnoitre, and brought back valuable information many a time.'

With Holck in Russia.

Von Richthofen remained with the 69th Flying Squadron until August 1915, participating in Mackensen's advance from Gorlice to Brest-Litovsk. His training as a cavalryman stood him in good stead and he took great enjoyment from taking part in long reconnaissance flights nearly every day.

'It is important for an observer to find a pilot with a strong character. One day we were told "Count Holck will join us." I thought immediately, "That's the man I want."

Holck made his appearance, not as one might imagine, in a 60h.p. Mercedes, or first-class sleeping car. He came on foot. After traveling by railway for days, he had reached the vicinity of Jaroslav. Here he got out and rather than endure yet another lengthy stoppage, told his orderly to travel on with the luggage while he continued on foot. After an hour of marching along the track, the train had still not caught up, so he continued walking. Thirty miles on he reached Rawa Ruska, his objective. Twenty-four hours later his orderly appeared with the luggage. He was so fit that the trek proved no difficulty to this sportsman.

Count Holck was not only a sportsman on land. To him, flying also was a sport, which gave him great pleasure. He was a pilot of rare talent and towered head and shoulders above the enemy. We went on many beautiful reconnaissance flights far into Russia. Although Holck was so young, I never felt insecure. In fact, during critical moments, he always supported me, for when I looked around and saw the determination in his face it always gave me twice as much courage.

My last flight with him nearly led to trouble. We had not had definite orders to fly but the glorious thing with the flying service is that you are your own master as soon as you take to the air.

We had to change our flying base and were not quite certain which meadow we were to land in. In order not to expose our machine to too much risk, we flew in the direction of Brest-Litovsk. The Russians were retreating everywhere and the whole countryside was burning. Our intention was to determine which direction the enemy columns were moving. This took us over the burning town of Wicznice. A gigantic smoke cloud ascending up to 6,000 feet stood in our way. I advised him to fly around, which would have added a five-minute detour, but Holck was more attracted to the greater danger of flying straight through! I enjoyed it too, but the venture nearly cost us dear.

No sooner had our tail disappeared within the smoke then the plane began to reel. I could not see a thing, for the smoke made my eyes water. The air was much warmer and beneath us was nothing but a huge sea of fire. Suddenly, the machine lost its balance and fell, turning round and round. I managed to grasp a stay and hung on to it to stop myself from being thrown out of the machine. The first thing I did was to look at Holck and the iron confidence etched across his face helped me to regain my courage. The only thought I had was: "how stupid it would be to die a hero's death so unnecessarily." Later, I asked Holck what his thoughts had been at that moment. He answered that he had never experienced such an unpleasant feeling.

We fell to an altitude of 1,500 feet above the burning town, it was either the skill of my pilot or a higher will — perhaps both — for as we dropped out of the smoke cloud, our good Albatros found itself again and flew once more straight ahead as if nothing had happened.

That was enough excitement for one day, and instead of going to our new base, we returned to our old quarters as fast as we could. After all, we were still above the Russians, and at an altitude of only 1,500 feet. Five minutes later Holck, said: "The motor is giving out." I must say that Holck had less knowledge of motors than he had of horseflesh, and since I knew even less about mechanics, I began to worry that if the motor went on strike, we would have to land among the Russians. So one peril had followed the other.

I was convinced that the Russians were still marching with energy. I could see them quite clearly from our low altitude. Besides, it was not necessary to look, for the Russians were shooting at us with machine-guns. The firing sounded like chestnuts roasting on a fire. Soon the motor stopped running altogether. It had been hit. We just managed to glide over a forest and landed in an abandoned artillery position, which the evening before, had still been occupied by Russians.

We jumped out and rushed towards the forest nearby, where we might be able to defend ourselves. I had a pistol and six cartridges. Holck had nothing. Once we had reached the safety of the wood, we stopped and were horrified to see a soldier running towards our plane through my binoculars. He wore not a spiked helmet but a cap, so I felt sure he was Russian, but as the man drew nearer, Holck shouted with joy for he recognised him as a Grenadier from the Prussian Guards. It transpired that our troops had stormed the Russian lines at the break of day and broken through into the enemy batteries.'

Russia to Ostend – from the two-seater to twin-engined fighter

The German offensive in Russia gradually came to a halt, and aircrews, including von Richthofen, were transferred to Ostend, Belgium, to train on a new twin-engined reconnaissance aircraft, Manfred, now 23, arrived there on 21st August 1915.

'I was tempted there by the name "Large warplane" and met my old friend Zeumer. I had a very good time during this part of my service. I saw little of the war but the experience was invaluable, for I passed my apprenticeship in aerial combat. We flew a great deal, but had no successes because we rarely had to fight in the air. We had occupied a hotel on the Ostend seafront, and bathed there every afternoon. Wrapped up in our many-colored gowns, we sat on the terrace in the afternoons drinking coffee

One day, this tranquillity was broken by the sound of bugles. We were told that a fleet of English boats was approaching. Of course, we did not allow ourselves to be alarmed and continued drinking until someone called out: "There they are!" We could just make out smoking funnels on the horizon, and fetched our telescopes. There was indeed quite an imposing fleet of vessels. We went to the roof to get a better view because It was not clear what they intended to do until the first shell came whistling through the air and exploded with a big bang on the very part of the beach where we had been bathing a little time before. I have never rushed so rapidly into the cellar as I did at that moment!

The English ships shot three or four times at us and then began bombarding the harbour and railway station. Of course they hit nothing, but the attack gave the Belgians a terrible fright. The only damage sustained was one shell that landed right on the beautiful Palace Hotel on the seafront, but since this belonged to Englishmen, the attack only destroyed English collateral!'

'During one of our training flights from Ostend, we went far out across the English Channel in our aircraft. We were experimenting with a new rudder system, which, we were told, would enable us to fly in a straight line with only a single engine working.

When we were fairly far out, I saw a ship beneath us, not on the water but below the surface. It seemed at first that it was traveling above the water, but when the sea is quiet, you can see clearly through several hundred metres of water. I had not made a mistake and drew Zeumer's attention to it and went lower to see more clearly. I am no naval expert but the ship appeared to be a submarine. But what nationality? Submarines do not carry a flag of course and one can scarcely distinguish colours under water. We had a couple of bombs with us and I debated whether to throw them or not. The submarine had not seen us and we might have flown above it without danger, waited for it to come to the surface, and then dropped our eggs. Here lies a dilemma for our sister arm.

When we had fooled around for quite a while I suddenly noticed the water in one engine was gradually disappearing. This was not good and I drew Zeumer's attention to it. He pulled a long face and turned for home. When we were still about 12 miles from shore, the engines began running more slowly and I prepared for a sudden cold dunk. That would almost certainly have been the case but for the new steering system we were testing, for our plane managed to continue under one engine and we landed close to the harbour without difficulty. We were very lucky, for with the old system, we would almost certainly have drowned.'

A Drop of Blood for the Fatherland

'I have never really been wounded. At critical moments I must have probably bent my head or pulled in my chest. It certainly surprises me that I have not been hit. Once, a bullet went through both of my fur-lined boots. Another time, one went through my muffler and on a further occasion, one went up the sleeve of my leather jacket, but I have never been touched'.

First aerial combat (1st Sept. 1915)

'Zeumer and I had great faith in our new twin-engined machine and were anxious to engage in a fight. We flew from Ostend for 5-6 hours every day without ever seeing an Englishman, which I found quite discouraging until one morning I spotted a Farman aeroplane reconnoitring the ground below. The pilot had not noticed us, and my heart beat furiously when Zeumer turned towards it. What was going to happen? I had never witnessed a fight in the air before and could not have been more vague about what to do. Before I knew it, the two planes rushed by each other. I managed to fire four shots at most before the Englishman was suddenly behind us, firing like mad. I never felt any sense of danger because I had no idea how the result might pan out. We twisted and turned around each another until, to our great surprise, the Englishman broke away and flew off. It was a great disappointment.

Returning home, we were both in very bad spirits. Zeumer reproached me for having shot badly, and I reproached him for not having enabled me to shoot well. In short, our relations, which had previously been faultless, suffered severely. We looked at our machine and discovered that it had received a respectable number of hits. I felt very sad. I had imagined that things would be very different. I had always believed that one shot would cause the enemy to fall, but now realised that a flying machine can stand a great deal of punishment.

We did not lack courage, Zeumer was a wonderful flier and I was quite a good shot. We stood before a riddle and were not the only crews to be left puzzled. Many even now, find themselves in the same position that we were in then and have to learn that this flying business must first be thoroughly understood.'

First blood

The good days in Ostend came to an abrupt end when von Richthofen's unit was ordered to the French Front to take part in the battle of Champagne. Enemy action at last, but they soon found that their large twin-engined aircraft were a poor match against more nimble Allied fighters.

'I flew once with Osteroth who had a smaller plane than the big apple carts we were flying. Three miles behind the Front, we encountered a Farman two-seater. Our opponent probably did not notice us until we approached him, and for the first time, I saw an aerial opponent close up. Osteroth flew with great skill side by side with the enemy so that I could easily fire at him, and it was only when I had trouble with my gun did he begin to shoot back at us.

When I had exhausted my supply of 100 bullets I noticed our opponent going down in curious spirals. I followed him with my eyes and tapped Osteroth's head to draw his attention. Our opponent dropped into a large crater. There he was, his machine standing on its head, the tail pointing towards the sky. According to the map he had fallen 3 miles behind the Front. We had

Circa 1915: German ace *Hauptmann* Boelcke, with a Fokker E.III in the background. Oswald Boelcke (19 May 1891–28 October 1916) was one of the most influential patrol leaders and tacticians during the early years of aerial warfare and became a father figure to Germany's fighter pilots. He went on to formalize the rules of air fighting which he presented as the Dicta Boelcke and promulgated rules for the individual pilot. His main concern, however, governed the use of formation fighting, rather than battles between individuals. Von Richthofen was taught by Boelcke and continued to idolize his late mentor long after he had surpassed Boelcke's tally of victories. Boelcke was credited with 40 aerial victories but died from injuries sustained during a relatively soft crash-landing because of his reluctance to wear a lap belt or helmet *therefore brought him down behind enemy lines. There was no way to verify it, otherwise I would have one more victory to my credit. But I was very proud of my success. After all, the chief thing is to bring a fellow down. It does not matter at all whether one is credited for it or not '.*

Meeting *Leutnant* Boelcke

Zeumer, von Richthofen's pilot, graduated to a single-seater Fokker monoplane which left Manfred to 'sail through the world alone'. As the Battle of Champagne raged, the French fliers had the upper hand and it was during a train journey to join another squadron on 1st October 1915 that he had a fortuitous meeting with a pilot who made quite an impression.

'A young, insignificant looking lieutenant was sitting in the dining car at the table next to me. There was no reason to take any notice of him except for the fact that he was the only man to have shot down hostile aircraft, not once but four times. His name had been mentioned in dispatches. I wanted to find out how Lieutenant Boelcke managed his business, so I asked him: "Tell me. How do you manage it? "He seemed very amused and replied: "Well it is quite simple. I fly close to my man, aim well, and then of course he falls down."

I shook my head and told him that I did the same thing but my opponents did not go down. The difference between us was that he flew a Fokker and I a large reconnaissance machine.

I took great trouble to get more closely acquainted with this nice modest fellow who I badly wanted to teach me his business. We often played cards together, went for walks and I asked him questions. I decided that I would also learn to fly a Fokker, and then perhaps my own chances would improve.

I now concentrated on learning how to manipulate the joystick myself and soon found an opportunity to learn piloting on an old machine in the Champagne. I threw myself into the work and after 25 training flights, stood before the examiner ready to fly alone.'

Royal Aircraft Factory FE.2b, 5203. It was an aircraft of this type that became Von Richthofen's first aerial victim on 17 September 1916.

Sopwith Pup B6088. A predecessor of the famed Sopwith Camel, the lightweight Pup, though somewhat under gunned, was an agile and effective scout (fighter) when it arrived on the Western Front in late 1916 where it out-performed many of the then-current German fighters. The origin of the name 'Pup' is far from certain, but the story goes that overjoyed pilots thought the machine was a derivative of the much larger Sopwith 1½ Strutter. A Pup became Von Richthofen's sixteenth victim on 4 January 1917.

Chapter Three

First Solo Flights

There are moments in life that set the nerves tingling. Taking a first solo flight is one of them. On the evening of 10th October 1915, Zeumer, von Richthofen's teacher, told him 'Now go and fly by yourself. Manfred was aged twenty-three and had received just 10 days of pilot training. By all accounts, it was a nerve-wracking moment.

> 'I felt like saying "I'm afraid", but this could never be said by a man defending his Country. Like it or not, I had to make the best of it and get into my machine. Zeumer ran through the basics once more, but I scarcely heard a word. I was convinced I would forget half of what he was telling me. I started the machine. The plane went off at the prescribed speed, and moments later, I found that I was actually flying. I felt elated. I did not care for anything and had complete contempt for death. I made a long curve to the left and flew round a tree, exactly as I had been told. Then came the difficult bit – landing.
>
> I remembered exactly what movements I had to make but the machine moved quite differently to what I expected. I lost my balance, made some wrong movements, and the plane finished up standing on its head. I had succeeded in converting my plane into a battered school bus. I was very sad. The damage done to the machine was not very great, but I had to suffer from everyone's jokes'.

It was back to training, and two days later, Manfred's confidence returned. He could handle the machine. A fortnight later, he took his examination:

> 'I described the figure-of-eight manoeuvre several times, exactly as I had been told, landed several times with success and felt very proud of my achievements. But to my great surprise, I was told that I had not passed. There was nothing to be done but to try once more to pass the initial examination.'

Training at Doberitz

Von Richthofen was sent to Berlin to complete his training and on 15th November 1915, flew to Doberitz as an observer in what to him was a 'giant plane'. The experience reinforced his belief that these gigantic machines would be no match against smaller planes in aerial combat. He was joined on the course by *Leutnant* von Lyncker and both became determined to fly Fokkers on the Western Front. A year later they succeeded in working together for a short time until a bullet caught his friend while bringing down his third plane.

While training in Doberitz, the two passed many hours away together. One of the things they had to do was to land in strange places, and Manfred took the opportunity to combine the necessary with the agreeable. His favourite landing place was on the Buchow estate where he was invited to shoot wild boar. He juggled his training commitments by taking a pilot with him on fine evenings as an observer, and touching down near the shoot. The second pilot then flew back to Doberitz and returned the following morning to pick von Richthofen up again.

'If I had not been collected by plane I would have been in a hole, for I would have had to march the 6 miles back to base. I required a pilot who would fetch me in any weather, which was not always easy. One night, a tremendous snowfall set in. I could not see more than 50 metres ahead. My pilot was due to fetch me at 8:00am sharp and for once, I hoped that he would not come. But suddenly I heard a humming noise – one could not see a thing – and 5 minutes later my beloved bird was squatting before me on the ground. Unfortunately some of her bones had got bent.'

Circa 1916: The Nieuport 17, a French fighter progressively developed from the earlier Nieuport 11 and 16 models. Equipped (generally) with a single machine gun, the Nieuport 17 first appeared over the Western Front in March or April 1916 and remained in widespread use until mid-1917, beyond which it became increasingly outclassed by a later generation of powerful twin-gun German fighters. Often described as a biplane, which of course it was, the Nieuport 17 was more accurately termed a sesquiplane (literally one-and-a-half wings), with the lower one being the smaller of the two. The image seen here is a little unusual in that eight steel tubes are attached to the outer struts which accommodated the La Prieur rocket – first introduced to battle in April 1916. Fired electrically, these rockets were intended to destroy the hydrogen-filled observation balloons used by Germany along the Western Front, a perilous undertaking given the balloons were heavily defended by guns on the ground plus standing fighter patrols, through which the attacking pilot had to get within 120 yards of his target for the rockets to have a chance to hit their goal.

Pilot von Richthofen

Manfred finally passed his pilot's examination at the third attempt on Christmas Day 1915, and went on to join the 2nd Battle Squadron at Verdun the following March where he flew two-seaters.

His first official mention in despatches came on 6th April. He was not named, but his deeds were. Von Richthofen had mounted a machine gun to his aircraft in a similar way to how the French and British mounted them above the top wing prior to the introduction of interrupter gear, which allowed guns to be fired through the arc of a revolving propeller. Its primitiveness led to a lot of ribbing from his own side until its effectiveness was proved against the enemy.

'I encountered a hostile Nieuport machine piloted by a man who was also a beginner, for he acted extremely foolishly. When I flew towards him he ran away, apparently because he had trouble with his gun. I had no idea of fighting him but thought: "What will happen if I now start shooting?" I flew after him, approached as closely as possible and began firing a short series of well-aimed bursts with my machine gun. The Nieuport reared up in the air and turned over and over. At first, both my observer and I both thought this was one of the tricks that French fliers habitually play. But the tricks did not cease. Turning over and over, the machine went lower and lower until crashing into a forest behind Fort Douaumont. It became clear to me that I had shot him down, but on the other side of the Front. I flew home and reported that I had shot down a Nieuport, which was reported in official despatches but does not count within the 52 aircraft that I have officially brought down to-date.'

Death of a mentor

On 30th April 1916, von Richthofen was again flying over Fort Douaumont when he noticed a Fokker attacking three French Caudron machines. Strong head winds made it impossible for him to join in, and he had to watch the fight unfold. To start with, the German pilot appeared to hold the upper hand, but then seven more French fighters arrived to redress the balance. Their combined assaults forced the Fokker pilot lower and lower until he was only 1,800 feet above Verdun. Suddenly, the German plane appeared to dive into a low cloud and seemingly escaped.

Back at the airfield, Manfred learned that the pilot of the Fokker was his comrade and mentor Count Holck who had crashed, after being shot in the head.

'His death deeply affected me. He had been my role model. He was a man among men, quite a character, and I had tried to imitate his energy.'

Thunderstorms

During the summer of 1916, flying was disturbed by frequent thunderstorms. There is nothing more disagreeable to a pilot than to fly through one, and during the Battle of the Somme later in the War, one of these localised storms brought down an entire British squadron behind German lines simply because they had been surprised by its ferocity, and the pilots spent the rest of the war as prisoners.

Von Richthofen's first such experience came while operating from an airfield at Metz. He found the challenge impossible to ignore.

'I was intending to return to my own base at Mont and was pulling my machine out of the hangar when the first signs of an approaching thunderstorm became noticeable. The clouds looked more like a gigantic black wall and older, more experienced pilots urged me not to fly. But I had promised to return to my base and would have considered myself a coward if I had failed to come back because of a silly thunderstorm. I intended to try.

As I started, the rain began falling and I had to take off my goggles in order to see anything. The problem was that I had to fly over the Moselle mountains which is where the thunderstorm was raging. I flew at the lowest possible altitude and very quickly, the gale seized my machine, driving it along as if it were a piece of paper. I was surrounded by an inky blackness. Suddenly I saw a wooded hill right in front of me. My Albatros managed to clear it, and from then on I had to clear every obstacle as I encountered it. The flight became a jumping competition over trees, villages, spires and steeples, for I could only fly in a straight line and had to keep within a few metres of the ground, otherwise I should have seen nothing at all.

Lightning playing all around and I did not know then that it could not affect planes. Death seemed inevitable, with the gale likely to throw me at any moment into a village or a forest. Had the motor stopped, I was done for. Just as suddenly I saw light on the horizon and concentrating all my energy, I steered towards it. The rain was still falling in torrents when I landed back at my airfield where everyone was waiting for me. Metz had reported my start and had told them that I had been swallowed up by the thundercloud.

I shall never again fly through a thunderstorm unless the Fatherland demands it of me, but looking back, the experience was very beautiful, a glorious moment I would not have wanted to miss.'

First time in a Fokker monoplane

From the outset, von Richthofen's burning ambition was to fly a single-seat fighter, and after harassing his Commander for some time, he finally got his wish to fly the new Fokker monoplane. He was to share it with fellow pilot Reimann, with Manfred taking it up in the morning, and his friend in the afternoon. Both were concerned that the other would smash it up.

Von Richthofen had the controls for the first morning but failed to find any enemy aircraft to attack, and returned safely. Reimann took his turn in the afternoon but failed to return. That evening an infantry report of an aerial battle between a Nieuport and a Fokker confirmed his fears. The German plane had been forced to land at Mort Homme, behind enemy lines, and the Squadron commemorated their brave comrade.

Then, in the middle of the night, the airfield received word that a German flying officer had made an unexpected appearance in the front trenches at Mort Homme. It transpired that Reimann's plane had been forced down after its engine had been hit by a bullet, and unable to land behind his own lines, he had come down in No Man's Land between the two fronts. He had set fire to the machine, then hidden in a mine crater until nightfall before crawling across to the German line.

A few days later, von Richthofen was given the opportunity to fly another Fokker monoplane. He too suffered engine failure and crash-landed in a field.

'In a moment the beautiful machine was reduced to a mass of scrap metal. It was a miracle that I was not hurt.'

Chapter Four

Bombing in Russia

In June 1916 orders came through for von Richthofen's squadron to load their planes on a train, no one knew where they were going, and it was only after crossing the whole of Germany that they were told of their destination – the Russian Front.

'Our time was spent annoying the Russians, dropped our eggs on their finest railway establishments. One day the whole squadron went out to bomb a very important railway station at Manjewicze, 18 miles behind the Front. The Russians were planning an attack and the station

Although intended initially for use as an 'eye in the sky' (i.e. reconnaissance) it wasn't long before aircraft were used more offensively. Unsurprisingly, and of necessity, the earliest form of bomb delivery on either side was extremely crude! The rank insignia on the man's epaulette seen here is that of a Royal Navy lieutenant.

was crammed with long lines of trains. For a time, I was delighted with bomb throwing. It gave me great pleasure to bomb those fellows from above.

That day, everything was ready. Each pilot tried his engine, for it is painful to be forced to land on the wrong side of the Front. The Russians hated us flyers, and if they caught a pilot they would certainly kill him. That is the only risk one ran in Russia, for the Russians have no aviators, or practically none. If a Russian flying man turned up he was sure to be shot down. The anti-aircraft guns used by Russia were sometimes quite good, but they were too few in number. Flying in the East is an absolutely holiday compared to flying over the Western Front.

Our planes, loaded to capacity, rolled heavily across the ground. Sometimes, I dragged 150 kg of bombs inside my C-machine, but then I had a very heavy observer too, who apparently had not suffered from the food shortages. Flying these heavy machines is no fun, especially during the mid-day summer heat in Russia. The plane sways about in a very disagreeable manner and the thought of carrying such a large quantity of explosives and benzene was not a pleasant one. But throwing bombs gave me a good deal of pleasure. It is splendid to be able to fly in a straight line and have a definite object in mind. When the bombs have gone one has the feeling that one has achieved something. In a fighter plane, you come home with a sense of failure if you fail to find an enemy plane to attack.

The run to Manjewicze is very pleasant. We passed over giant forests probably inhabited by elks and lynxes, but the villages looked miserable. The only substantial town was Manjewicze. It was surrounded by tents, and countless barracks had been run up near the railway station. We could not make out the Red Cross.

Another flying squadron had visited the place before us and had not done badly. The exit of the station was blocked by a lucky hit on an engine that was still steaming. The driver had probably dived into a shelter. On the other side of the station, an engine was just coming out and we dropped a bomb a few hundred metres ahead, which had the desired effect. We turned and continued throwing bomb after bomb on the station, I taking careful aim through our telescope. We had plenty of time for nobody interfered with us. An enemy airfield was in the neighbourhood but there was no trace of hostile pilots. A few anti-aircraft guns were busy, but not shooting in our direction, and we reserved one last bomb hoping to make particularly good use of it against them on our way home. As we approached the airfield, I noticed an enemy flying machine starting out from its hangar. The question was whether it would attack us? I did not believe so. It was more likely that the pilot was seeking security in the air, for when bombers are about, the air is the safest place.

We went home by a roundabout route looking for camps. It was amusing to pepper the gentlemen below with our machine guns and particularly interesting to shoot at hostile cavalry. An aerial attack upsets them completely, and they rush away in all directions. I would not like to be the Commander of a lot of Cossacks that have been machine gunned from the air. By and by we recognised the German lines, and still to dispose of our last bomb, we resolved to make a present of it to a Russian observation balloon team. It was the only balloon they possessed. We descended to within a few hundred feet of the ground and the Russians began to haul it in very rapidly. Once the bomb had been dropped the hauling stopped. I don't believe that I hit it, but imagine that the Russians ran away, leaving their chief in the air!

Although this example is a German observation balloon, they made ideal aerial platforms for intelligence gathering and artillery spotting. During World War One most of the warring nations employed them, generally a few miles behind the front lines. Such balloons were fabric envelopes filled with hydrogen, the inflammable nature of which led to the destruction of hundreds on both sides. Observers were frequently issued with parachutes to allow a rapid exit from the balloon as soon as an enemy fighter attack appeared to be imminent in order to avoid the flammable consequences of hydrogen. Typically, balloons were tethered to a steel cable attached to a winch that reeled the gasbag to its desired height (often above 3,000 feet) and retrieved it at the end of an observation session.

Another time in the same neighbourhood, we were ordered to meet a Russian attack intent on crossing the River Stokhod. We arrived laden with bombs and a large number of cartridges for our machine guns, and found their cavalry already crossing over the single bridge. It was clear that we could do tremendous harm to the enemy by hitting the bridge.

Dense masses of men were crossing. We went as low as possible and could clearly see the cavalry crossing with great rapidity. The first bomb fell near the bridge. The second and third followed immediately after, and created tremendous disorder. The bridge had not been hit but traffic across it ceased completely. Men and animals were rushing away in all directions. My observer fired energetically into the crowd and we enjoyed it tremendously. I cannot say what success we had but imagine that we caused the Russian attack to fail. Perhaps the official account in the Russian War Office will give me details after the war.

I was never able to make proper use of our machine guns against enemy planes in Russia and regret that my collection of trophies contains does not a single Russian kill.'

Recruited by Boelcke

It was August and unbearably hot in the sun drenched sandy airfield at Kovel. Von Richthofen and his squadron were continuing to make their bombing sorties over the Russian lines almost with impunity, and the flying crews were getting great satisfaction from it. Then, word spread that the German flying ace Oswald Boelcke was to drop in while returning from Turkey.

'Boelcke arrived on a visit to us, or rather to his brother. He was vastly admired and told us many interesting things about his journey to Turkey. He expected to go back to the Somme to organize a fighting squadron and was selecting men from the flying corps who seemed to him to be best skilled at flying fighter planes. I did not dare to ask him. I did not feel at all bored by the fighting in Russia, but the idea of fighting again on the Western Front attracted me. There is nothing better for a young cavalry officer than the chase.

Boelcke was due to leave us the following morning, and quite early there was a knock on my door. There stood the great man wearing his Order Pour le Mérite medal. He had come to ask me if I was interested in becoming his pupil and join him at the Somme. I almost fell around his neck.'

Three days later von Richthofen was on a train travelling through Germany, straight to the Western Front to join the newly formed *Jagdstaffel* 2 (*Jasta*) fighter squadron based at Lagnicourt, feeling that his greatest wish was to be fulfilled. This, he thought, was the start to the finest time of his life.

The Battle of the Somme – First kill.

On September 17, 1916, in his first trip in a combat patrol commanded by Boelcke, von Richthofen found himself and his Albatros biplane engaged in aerial combat with a plane piloted by British Second Lieutenant Lionel Bertram Frank Morris.

Their aircraft was an FE.2b, one of six sent up to provide a fighter cover for eight defenceless BE.2ds from 12 Squadron on a bombing mission over the railway station at Marcoing near Cambria. The bombers were so laden with explosives that they had to fly without gunners, and it was their misfortune that this would be the first day that Oswald Boelcke's Jagdstaffel 2 had

1916: A British plane brought down in flames behind German lines on the Western Front. In the background is a German Albatros D.III biplane. Victorious pilots such as von Richthofen would land close to their victim if possible, both to cast an eye for any technical advancements on the fallen machine, or to take a small piece from the plane as a trophy. Von Richthofen covered his wall with serial numbers cut from the fuselage of his fallen rivals.

enough aircraft to put a true fighting unit together and begin to operate as its leader had thought a fighting unit should.

The German group took to the skies to patrol the area around Marcoing at the same time as the two British squadron flights, which encountered severe anti-aircraft fire (Archie as it was known) as they crossed the lines. The bombers dropped their bombs shortly after 10:30am but then all hell broke loose as Boelcke's group of young pilots swept in to intercept. Soon, they had shot down four of the six fighter planes from 11 Squadron and two of the eight bombers from No 12.

The ungainly looking FE.2bs were pusher aircraft with the engine and propeller mounted behind the pilot and observer's seats. This arrangement gave the observer, who was not strapped in, the freedom of movement to fire his Lewis machine gun forwards as well as backwards over the top of the wing. Von Richthofen had been quick to learn that the weak point of the FE.2b was underneath and had come up from below the plane piloted by Morris.

Richthofen recounted the experience:

'I detected shrapnel clouds in the direction of Cambra and hurried forth. I met a squad that I attacked shortly after 1100. I singled out the last machine. My Englishman twisted and turned, flying in zigzags. I was driven by a single thought: 'The man in front of me must come down,

whatever happens.' At last a favourable moment arrived. My opponent had apparently lost sight of me. Instead of twisting and turning, he flew straight along. In a fraction of a second I was on him. I fired several times at close range, getting so close that I was afraid I might dash into the Englishman. Suddenly I nearly yelled with joy, for the enemy's propeller stopped turning. Hurrah! I had shot his engine to pieces; the enemy was compelled to land. It was impossible for him to reach his own lines. The machine glided down and I followed until I had killed the observer who had not stopped shooting until the last moment.

To ensure that his first success would be recorded, von Richthofen landed alongside his stricken enemy in time to see Morris being pulled out of the cockpit and taken away to hospital where he died. To mark this first 'kill', von Richthofen had a small silver cup engraved with the details – something he would repeat for each successive victory until the jeweller ran out of silver, long before his client ran out of victories.

Morris had become an articled clerk at Inns on the Court, London in May 1915 after graduating from Whitgift School, Croydon. He gained his pilot's certificate in January the following year, and had only 9 months active flying service before meeting his death at the hand of von Richthofen.

Circa 1916: German flying aces. Left to right, Oswald Boelcke, Hermann Kastner and Max Immelmann. The three men were the father figures of the German Air Force and had a huge influence over Manfred von Richthofen's career as a fighter pilot.

He was aged just 19. He and Lieutenant Rees, a 21 year old Welsh recruit from Brecon, were both buried with full military honours at the Porte-de-Paris cemetery, Cambrai.

Having gained his first 'kill' von Richthofen relished the opportunity to shoot down more enemy planes.

'I have not found a happier hunting ground than during the course of the Somme battle. The first Englishmen arrived as soon as I had got up in the morning and the last did not disappear until long after sunset. Boelcke once described it as a flying man's "El Dorado!"

Within two months, Boelcke's bag had increased from 20 to 40. We beginners did not have his experience and were quite satisfied when we did not get a hiding. It was an exciting period. Every time we went up we had a fight. Frequently, we fought really big battles in the air, sometimes against 40 to 60 English planes. The Germans were often in the minority but with us, quality was more important than quantity. But the Englishman is a smart fellow and sometimes visited Boelcke in his quarters, coming down to a very low altitude and throwing their bombs at us. They challenge us continually, never refusing a fight.

We had a delightful time in our fighter squadron. The spirit of our leader inspired all his pupils and we trusted him blindly. There was no possibility of one of us being left behind, and with this spirit, we gladly went up to diminish enemy numbers.'

Boelcke's death

'On 18th October 1916 we were flying with Boelcke against the enemy. We always had a wonderful feeling of security when he was with us. The weather was very gusty and there were many clouds. Some distance away, we saw two Englishmen in the air who seemed to be enjoying the terrible weather. There were six of us against their two. The fight began in the usual way. Boelcke tackled one and I the other. I had to break off when one of the German planes got in my way, and looking around, I noticed Boelcke setting up his victim some 200 metres away. It was the usual thing. Boelcke would shoot down his opponent and I had to look on.

Close to Boelcke was his good friend Lieutenant Erwin Böhme and both were shooting. It looked likely that the Englishman would fall at any moment. But then I noticed the two German flying machines go into an unnatural movement. My first thought was they had collided. I had not witnessed a collision in the air before and had imagined it would look quite different. The two machines had simply touched one another. Boelcke drew away and began to descend in wide curves. He did not seem to be falling until I noticed that part of his plane had broken off. He became lost in the cloud and I did not see what happened, but his machine was no longer steerable and as it fell, Boelcke's plane was accompanied down by his faithful friend. When we returned to base, the report 'Boelcke is dead' had already arrived. We could scarcely believe it. The greatest pain was of course felt by the man who had the misfortune to be involved in the accident.

It is a strange thing that anyone who met Boelcke imagined that they were his true friend. I have met about 40 men who believed they had a monopoly on his affections – even men whose names were unknown to him. This is a curious phenomenon that I have not noticed with anyone else. Boelcke had no personal enemies and was equally polite to everybody. The only one who was perhaps closest to him was the very man who had the misfortune to be in the accident that caused his death. Nothing happens without God's will. That is the only consolation that any of us can put to our souls during this war."

The body of Lieutenant Quentin Roosevelt, 95th Aero Squadron, American Expeditionary Force. Born on 19 November 1897, Quentin Roosevelt was the youngest son of President Theodore Roosevelt. He was killed in aerial combat over France on Bastille Day (14 July 1918) and is seen here lying dead beside his Nieuport 28 fighter. Family and friends agreed that Quentin had many of his father's positive qualities and few of the negative ones. Inspired by his father and siblings, he joined the Air Service of the United States Army in which he became a pursuit (fighter) pilot. Extremely popular with his fellow pilots and known for his daring, Quentin's aircraft was brought down during an aerial combat over Chamery, near Coulonges-en-Tardenois; two bullets having struck him in the head. The German military buried him with full honours and, since the plane had crashed so near the front lines, they used sections of his Nieuport to make a cross for his grave. For propaganda purposes the Germans made a postcard of the dead pilot and his plane!

Circa 1918: A gruesome photograph showing the badly burned bodies of two airmen following Richthofen's 74th kill. If correct, this image shows the remains of Second Lieutenants J. Taylor and E. Betley of No.82 Squadron RFC who were shot down in their Armstrong Whitworth FK8, C8444, on 28 March 1918 whilst conducting a reconnaissance.

My 8th victim

'During Boelcke's time, 8 'kills' was a respectable number. Those who hear of the colossal bags made by certain aviators nowadays, might think it has become easier to shoot down an enemy plane, but I can assure you that it is becoming more difficult by the month, and even week by week.

With the increasing number of planes there is of course an increase in the number of opportunities to shoot down an enemy. But at the same time, the possibility of being shot down oneself has also increased. Along with the increasing number of enemy planes, are improvements to the armaments they carry. When my colleague Immelmann shot down his first victim, he had the good fortune to find an opponent who did not even carry a machine gun. These days, such innocents can only be found on the training grounds.

On 9th November 1916, I flew towards enemy lines accompanied by Immelmann, then only 18 years old. We were both in Boelcke's squadron and got on very well. Comradeship is a most important thing. I had already bagged 7 enemy planes and Immelmann 5. At that time this was quite a lot. Soon after reaching the Front, we spotted a squadron of bombers. They arrived in enormous numbers 40 to 50 machines and had selected a target not far from our airfield. I engaged the last plane, shot the machine gunner and may even have tickled the pilot too for he decided to land with his bombs. I fired a few more shots to accelerate his progress and he fell close to our flying base at Lagnicourt.

Circa 1915: German air ace *Leutnant* Max Immelmann photographed next to the wreckage of one of his 15 victories. Immelmann (21 September 1890 -18 June 1916) was the first aviator to win the *Pour le Mérite* (Blue Max), which was awarded to him it at the same time as Oswald Boelcke.

Oberleutnant Immelmann †
(letzte Aufnahme)

610

Oberleutnant Max Immelmann flew in Oswald Boelcke's squadron with von Richthofen during the 1916 campaign in northern France against the British and influenced the way he fought in the air. Immelmann developed tactical rules for air combat and the use of formation fighting. He invented what became known as the 'Immelmann Turn' following a high-speed diving attack on an enemy. This turn involved climbing back up past the enemy aircraft, and just short of stalling, applying full rudder to yaw the aircraft around to face down at the enemy aircraft and follow through with a second high-speed dive in any direction. Immelmann was an early proponent of the gun synchroniser, which allowed the pilot to sight through the arc of its spinning propeller without bullets striking the blades. When killed on 18 June 1916, after his aircraft broke up in mid-air, it remained uncertain whether it was enemy fire or his own gun that shattered one blade of his propeller which caused the severe vibration that shook his plane to pieces.

Immelmann brought down another Englishman in the same locality and we flew home quickly to see the machines we had downed. It was very hot, and after jumping into a car to get closer to where our victims lay, we then had to run some distance through the fields to reach them. As I did so, I unbuttoned my collar and shirt and took off my jacket. My boots became covered in mud and by the time I arrived, I looked like a tramp. I approached a group of officers on the spot, greeted them, and asked one whether he could tell me anything about the aerial battle because it is always interesting to learn how a fight in the air looks to people on the ground. He told me that the English planes had thrown bombs and that this one that had come down still carrying its payload.

The officer then took my arm and introduced me to the other officers who all looked so spic and span that they might have come straight from the parade ground. I was embarrassed by my attire and during one conversation with an impressive person wearing General's trousers, I attempted to re-button my collar and shirt. I had no idea who the officer was and after taking my leave, returned home again. That evening the telephone rang and I was told that His Royal Highness, the Grand Duke of Saxe-Coburg Gotha had ordered to see me. It transpired that the English planes had intended to bomb his headquarters and that I apparently, had helped to keep them away. He presented me with the Saxe-Coburg Gotha medal for bravery.'

Major Hawker

Lanoe George Hawker VC, DSO (his image appears in the introduction) was a British flying ace, with seven credited victories, during the First World War. He was the first British flying ace, and only the third pilot to receive the Victoria Cross, the highest and most prestigious award for gallantry in the face of the enemy. The son of a distinguished military family, Hawker was born at Longparish, Hampshire, on 30 December 1890 and served at the Royal Military Academy in Woolwich before joining the Royal Engineers, as an officer cadet. A clever inventor, Hawker developed a keen interest in all mechanical and engineering developments, and was posted to France in October 1914, as a Captain with No.6 Squadron, Royal Flying Corps, flying Henri Farman planes. He was killed in a dogfight over the Somme against Manfred von Richthofen on 23rd November 1916.

'I felt extremely proud when informed that the airman I had brought down was the English Immelmann. In view of our fight, it was clear to me that I had been tackling a flying champion.

That day, I had noticed three Englishmen who appeared to want a fight, and did not want to disappoint them. I was flying at a lower altitude and had to wait until one of them tried to drop on me. After a short while one of the three attempted to tackle me from the rear but after firing five shots, had to stop when I swerved away in a sharp curve. The two of us circled round and round like madmen at an altitude of 10,000 feet, 20 turns to the left and then 30 to the right while trying to get behind and above the other. I soon realised that I had not met a beginner. He had no intention of breaking off the fight and was flying in a machine that turned beautifully. But my own plane was better at rising than his, and eventually, I succeeded in getting above my English waltzing partner.

Once we had dropped down to 6,000 feet, my opponent should have realised that it was time to take his leave for the wind was in my favour, blowing us towards the German line. However, when we were 3,000 feet above Bapaume, less than a mile behind the German Front, he had the cheek to wave at me as if to say, "Well, how do you do?" The circles we made around one another were probably no more than 100 metres, close enough for me to look down into his cockpit and see every movement of his head. My English rival was a good sportsman, but eventually things became a little too hot for him. He had to decide whether to land on German soil or attempt to fly back to English lines. Of course he tried the latter, having endeavoured in vain to escape by performing loops and other such tricks.

When he had come down to about 300 feet, he tried to escape by flying in a zigzag course during which it is difficult for an observer to shoot. That was my moment. I followed him at an altitude of between 150 to 250 feet, firing all the time. My opponent fell, shot through the head, 50 metres behind our line just as my gun jammed. His machine gun was dug out of the ground and now ornaments the entrance to my home.'

Chapter Five

My Own Squadron

Boelcke's death did nothing to dull von Richthofen's dedication to the cause. Indeed, the loss of his leader might have sharpened his appetite, for soon, Manfred had 16 kills to his credit and topped the German fighter pilots league table. But somehow, he felt forgotten. Where was his Order of Merit? Both Boelcke and Immelman had been presented with theirs after downing 8 aircraft.

One day a telegram arrived for Manfred and he opened it eagerly. It stated: LIEUTENANT VON RICHTHOFEN IS APPOINTED COMMANDER OF THE ELEVENTH FIGHTER SQUADRON (N.B. JAGDSTAFFEL 11)

His disappointment was clear to all. He wrote:

Herr Georg Michaelis, Imperial Chancellor from 13th July 1917 to 30th October 1917, talking to von Richthofen on the Somme Front. The ace became such a celebrity that high ranking officers often went out of their way to be photographed with him.

Circa 1917: Albatros D.IIIs of *Jagdstaffel* 11 and *Jagdstaffel* 4 parked in a line at La Brayelle near Douai, France. Manfred von Richthofen's red-painted aircraft is second in line.

'I was annoyed. I had learnt to work so well with my comrades in Boelcke's Squadron, and now I had to begin all over again working hand-in-hand with new people. I would have preferred the Order Pour le Merite.'

They must have heard back at HQ, for two days later, a second telegram arrived stating: HIS MAJESTY HAS GRACIOUSLY CONDESCENDED TO GIVE YOU THE ORDRE POUR LE MERITE. He soon warmed to the idea of commanding his own unit, and to mark the occasion, decided to have his own plane painted a flamboyant red.

'The result was that everyone got to know my red bird. Even my opponents noticed the colour transformation.

During a fight on a different section of the Front, I had the good fortune to shoot down a Vickers two-seater photographing German artillery positions. The crew did not have time to defend themselves. Their plane started to smoke and burst into flames as it was going down to earth. I felt some pity for them because I thought they must be wounded, and followed them down. Suddenly, at about 1,500 feet, I suffered engine trouble and had to land without making any curves. The result was comical. My enemy with their burning machine, landed smoothly while I, the victor, came down and overturned my plane into the barbed wire of our trenches next to them! Surprised by my collapse, the two Englishmen could not understand why I had landed so clumsily and greeted me like a sportsman. They were the first two Englishmen that I had brought down alive and it gave me particular pleasure to talk to them. I asked them whether they had seen my machine in the air before, and one of them replied, "Oh, yes. I know your machine very well. We call it Le Petit Rouge".'

English verses French character

By February 1917, von Richthofen's flyers were trying to compete with Boelcke's old squadron. Each evening they sat down and eagerly compared the number of kills, yet the other unit had a lead of more than 100 Allied aircraft downed, despite which, Manfred was determined that his men would catch up. He wrote:

'Everything depends on who we have for opponents: those French tricksters or the daring English. I prefer the English. Often, their daring can only be described as stupidity. The decisive factor does not lie in trick flying but the ability and energy of the aviator. A flying man may be able to loop and do all the stunts imaginable, yet not succeed in shooting down a single enemy plane. In my opinion, aggression is everything; a spirit that is very strong in us Germans. That is why we will always have domination in the air.

The French have a different character. They like to set traps and to surprise their opponents. This cannot easily be done in the air and only a beginner will be caught out. Sometimes, though, Gaelic blood asserts itself and the French will attack. But French attacking spirit is like bottled lemonade. It lacks tenacity. The English, on the other hand, have some German blood in them. They take to flying and see it as nothing more than a sport. They take delight in looping the loop, flying on their back, and indulging in other stunts for the benefit of our soldiers in the trenches. These tricks might impress people attending a sporting event, but do not impress on the battlefront where higher qualifications are required. That is why the blood of English pilots will flow in streams.'

A Home Defence (Northern Group) Avro 504K (single-seat adaptation) biplane manufactured by the Avro Aircraft Company. The Avro 504 was also built under licence by other manufacturers and over 10,000 were built from 1913 to the time production ended in 1932. Small numbers of early aircraft were purchased both by the Royal Flying Corps (RFC) and the Royal Naval Air Service (RNAS)* prior to the start of World War I, and were taken to France when the war started. After the War two-seat 504 variants became the RAF's standard trainer.

(* The Royal Flying Corps was the air arm of the British Army during the First World War until, on 1 April 1918, it was merged with the Royal Naval Air Service to form the Royal Air Force.)

Circa 1916: The Airco DH.2 was a single-seat biplane scout that utilised a 'pusher' engine, as opposed to the more usual tractor ('puller') layout, and was designed by Geoffrey de Havilland who based it on his earlier DH.1 two-seater. The DH.2 was the first British single-seat fighter to effectively incorporate a forward firing 'fixed' machine gun in front of the pilot – as opposed to those which employed a gun fitted above the centre section of the top wing to clear the arc of the propeller. It was the DH.2 that enabled RFC pilots to counter the 'Fokker Scourge' that had given the Germans the advantage in the air in late 1915. Until the British developed a gun synchronisation gear to match the German system, pushers such as the DH.2 and the F.E.2b two-seater carried the burden of fighting and escort duties over the Western Front. The DH.2 entered RFC service from February 1916 with No.24 Squadron.

An undated photograph of an RFC BE.2-series reconnaissance aircraft entangled in telephone wires on a railway embankment (presumably) somewhere in Britain circa 1916. BE.2 and BE.12 series reconnaissance aircraft were particularly vulnerable to enemy fighters, with many of their type falling to the guns of Richthofen himself – in fact he accounted for 20 of them.

Circa 1917: The G.100 'Elephant' bi-plane was, in its day, a very large single-seat fighter, one which approximated in size to a contemporary two-seater. Built by the British manufacturer Martinsyde (a contraction of Martin & Handasyde) the first G.100, serial number 4735, flew in September 1915. Thereafter, from early 1916, Elephants were attached piecemeal to various squadrons as escorts to their two-seaters, although at least one unit, No.27 Squadron, arrived in France in March 1916 equipped solely with the type. However, although the latter didn't make much of a name for itself as a fighter, its size, strength and endurance did allow it to carry a useful bomb load and as such it remained in use in Europe until late 1917, and in the Middle East until at least the Armistice of November 1918. The aircraft shown here, 7469, is a G.100 from the second production batch which went on to serve with No.27 Squadron and although the name Elephant was never officially adopted, an elephant has been incorporated into No.27 Squadron's badge ever since. Von Richthofen's second victory was a 27 Squadron G.100 which he destroyed on 23 September 1916.

Circa 1917: An RFC Nieuport 17 C1, hundreds of which served in the RFC/RAF. This French sesquiplane fighter designed by the Nieuport Company offered outstanding manoeuvrability and an excellent rate of climb, giving it a significant advantage over most other fighters of its day – on either side. Consequently, the model was widely used by every Allied power, and the design was even copied in Germany.

Sopwith's 1½ Strutter two-seat fighter-reconnaissance design derived its name from the '1½' pairs of struts joining each wing either side of the fuselage. Armed with a Lewis gun in the rear cockpit, the type was notable for being the first British aircraft to (generally) be equipped with a fixed, synchronised, machine gun for the pilot prior to entering service. RFC 1½ Strutters first appeared over the Western Front in or about May 1916 where they operated both in their intended role and reportedly as bombers too, carrying up to about 130lb of bombs. As a fighter it was outclassed by May 1917 and its withdrawal from the Western Front was completed in October 1917, some being removed to Home Defence units in the UK. However, it survived longer with the RNAS who frequently used it as a single-seat bomber, as a fighter and also to conduct a number of deck landing and take-off experiments. By early 1918 the type had largely been withdrawn from British operational service, but continued as a training aircraft to the end of the war and just beyond.

An undated image showing an RE.8 with damage to its starboard fuselage and top mainplane. The Royal Aircraft Factory RE.8 was a British two-seat biplane reconnaissance aircraft which also carried bombs if required. First flown on 17 June 1916, the first operational examples arrived in France with No.52 Squadron in the following November. Intended as a replacement for the venerable BE.2 series, the RE.8 soon gained an unhappy reputation within the RFC due to the many crashes that were recorded, mostly after spinning into the ground from low altitude – though many of these incidents were the result of grossly inadequate pilot training! However, improvements were made to both the machine and aircrew training so that, in capable hands, it became a reasonably satisfactory aircraft which could defend itself in combat – and often did so. In fact, on 21 April 1918, the day that Richthofen died, two RE.8s were attacked by four of Richthofen's fighters and ought to have been easy prey, however, gunfire from the two observers drove the fighters off – damaging two of them.5

The Sopwith triplane single-seat scout (fighter) entered operational service in 1917 and was nicknamed the 'Tripe'. Powered initially by an 110hp Clerget 9-cylinder rotary engine and later by a 130hp engine of the same type, it was operated by the Royal Naval Air Service (RNAS). Used almost exclusively over the Western Front, this design proved to be such a capable and highly manoeuvrable fighter that its success became measured by the number of German and Austrian triplane designs that materialised as a result of this fighter's achievements – the most notable of which was the Fokker Dr.I.

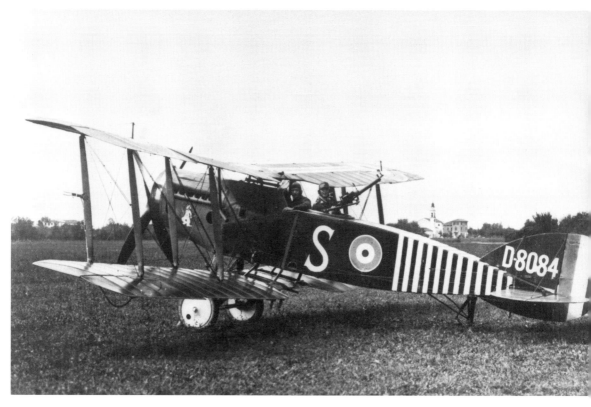

Bristol Fighter (F.2B) two-seat fighter, D8084, of No.139 Squadron photographed in Italy during 1918. The Bristol F.2 was operated by the RFC and the RAF during the First World War. Often simply referred to as the Bristol Fighter, 'Brisfit' or 'Biff' the F.2B, despite being a large two-seater, proved to be an agile aircraft fully able to hold its own against opposing single-seat fighters: only three Brisfits fell to the guns of the Red Baron – namely two F.2As and one F.2B. Its initial combat debut, however, ended poorly, but steadily thereafter squadrons began to employ the aircraft more offensively – much like single-seat scouts, albeit one protected by a rear gunner who was equipped with a Lewis machine gun, as shown in this image, but increasingly with twin Lewis guns to supplement the pilot's single (often twin) Vickers machine gun(s). The F.2B's solid design ensured that it remained in military service into the 1930s, while surplus machines were popular in civil aviation.

A pilot sits in the cockpit of a Sopwith biplane, a Camel with the aft end of its gun-breech fairing removed. This image clearly indicates the pilot's proximity to his pair of Vickers .303 machine guns with which this machine is equipped, the cocking handle of the left-hand gun being evident. Being so close to the guns was a desirable feature in several respects as it allowed pilots of the era, of any nation, to try and clear a gun stoppage – an all to frequent occurrence – as quickly as possible, often with the help of a mallet though how a pilot found room to swing one in the confines of a Camel's cockpit is open to question! In order to help prevent a gun from jamming in the first place, several fighter pilots only allowed their guns to be loaded after having personally examined every round of ammunition themselves as faulty ammo was the primary cause of stoppages, the likely consequences of which are obvious. Each gun belt (one per gun) carried 250 rounds. Other less obvious features seen here include a circular leather pad in front of the pilot's face, and an Aldis gunsight which extends through the base of the diminutive windscreen.

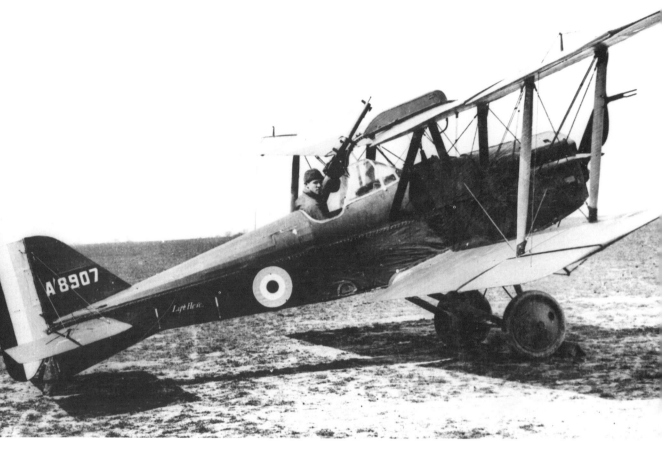

Circa 1917: The SE.5, and more particularly the later SE.5a along with the Sopwith Camel, became Britain's primary single-seat fighters from mid-1917 until the end of the war. Built in quantity, both types were the equal of enemy designs when flown in the hands of skilled pilots with both types being frequently encountered by German pilots, Richthofen included. This familiar image shows an early production SE.5 which, as with the great majority of the SE.5/5a series, was equipped with two machine guns: one mounted on the forward fuselage and the other on a Foster mounting atop the upper wing. Early SE.5s were fitted with a semi-enclosed cockpit canopy (seen here) – a universally disliked addition it would seem and they were quickly removed in operational service. The pilot seen here is Captain Albert Ball VC.

An Albatros D.III single-seat fighter. The Albatros D.III was a streamlined German single-seat fighter which first flew in December 1916 and was followed by the even more streamlined Albatros D.V and D.Va, both of which served until the end of the war.

An Albatros D.Va single-seat fighter biplane – serial number D.5390/17. The Albatros D.V entered service in May 1917 and, like the D.III before it, immediately began to experience structural failures of the lower wing. Indeed, anecdotal evidence suggests that the D.V was even more prone to wing failures than the D.III. The outboard sections of the upper wing also suffered failures and required additional wire bracing. Furthermore, the D.V offered very little improvement in performance. This caused considerable dismay among front line pilots, many of whom preferred the older D.III., Richthofen himself was particularly critical of the new aircraft. In a July 1917 letter, he described the D.V as 'so obsolete and so ridiculously inferior to the English that one can't do anything with this aircraft'. British tests of a captured D.V revealed that the aircraft was slow to manoeuvre, heavy on the controls, and tiring to fly. The response to such criticisms was the Albatros D.Va, which featured stronger wing spars, heavier wing ribs and a reinforced fuselage. Orders were placed for 262 D.Va aircraft in August 1917, followed by additional orders for 250 in September and 550 in October. Today D.5390/17 is displayed at the Australian War Memorial in Canberra.

Circa 1918: Richthofen pictured landing his Fokker Dr.I triplane after a patrol.

Circa 1917: Richthofen's all-red Fokker Dr.I triplane. This machine was originally powered with an 80hp Oberursel rotary engine, until replaced with an Oberursel Ur II rotary engine of 110hp – copied from the French Le Rhone engine.

Circa 1918: The work of Reinhold Platz – Anthony Fokker's chief designer – the Fokker D.VII was reputedly the best German fighter of the First World War; some argue that it was the finest fighter produced by any nation during that war. Whether it was or not remains unresolved, but whatever the truth, when the Allies dictated their surrender terms to a defeated Germany it was specified that all remaining D.VIIs be handed over to the Allies – proof if nothing else of this aircraft's prowess in capable hands! The design did have its faults, the worst being that there was not enough of them available between its entry into service in late April 1918 and the Armistice. Von Richthofen had criticised one of the early prototypes for being unstable, to which Fokker responded by improving the airframe, which was then tested in January 1918 by Richthofen and others.

Shot down

It was the middle of March 1917 that von Richthofen suffered his first set back in the air during an aerial battle over German artillery positions around Lens

'We were five; our English opponents were three times as many, and flying around like midges. An aggressive spirit is the chief thing anywhere in war, and the air is no exception. The enemy had the same and turned to attack as soon as they saw us. We five had to look sharp for should one of us fall, the rest would be in trouble. We went closer together and waited for the foreigners to approach us. We did not have to wait long. There! One of them is stupid enough to depart alone. He is within reach and I say to myself, "That man is lost."

I am after him. When I get near, he starts shooting prematurely, which shows that he is nervous. I think to myself, "Go on shooting – You won't hit me." He is firing tracer bullets that ignite so I see his shots passing me. I felt as if I were sitting in a giant watering can – not a pleasant sensation. Still, the English usually shoot these bullets, so we must get accustomed to it. One can get accustomed to anything.

I think I laughed out loud but was soon given a hard lesson. When I got to within 100 metres of him, I got ready to fire and aimed a few trial bursts. The machine guns were in order, and in my mind's eye, I saw my enemy dropping. The excitement had gone. I was thinking calmly and collectively, weighing up the probabilities of hitting or being hit. As a rule, the fight itself is the least exciting part of the business. The one who gets excited is sure to make mistakes. Calmness is a matter of habit. At any rate, I did not make a mistake. I closed to within 50 metres and fired. I thought I was bound to be successful. Then suddenly, I heard a tremendous bang. Something hit my machine. There was a fearful stench of benzene and then the engine slowed. The Englishman noticed it too, for he started shooting with redoubled energy.

I instinctively went into a dive and switched off the engine. When the benzene tank has been perforated and the infernal liquid is squirting around your legs, the danger of fire is very great. A single drop on the red-hot engine would be enough to set the machine in flames. Behind, I was leaving a thin trace of white cloud. I knew from watching my opponents go down, that this is the first sign of an explosion. I was still at 9,000 feet but descending at such a rate that I could no longer put my head out of the cockpit. I soon lost sight of my opponent. I had time only to glimpse at what my four comrades were doing. They were still fighting and I could hear their machine guns firing.

Then I notice a rocket. Was it an enemy signal? No, the light is too great for a rocket. It must be another plane, but from which side? It looks like one of our own. No! Praise the Lord, it is an enemy one! Who could have shot him down? Now another machine drops out, falling straight towards the ground, turning, turning, turning exactly as I had. But just as suddenly, it recovers its balance and flies straight towards me. It is another Albatros experiencing the same problems that I have, no doubt. Once down to 1,000 feet, I started to look for a landing place. Such landings usually lead to breakages. I found a meadow, not very large but it was just sufficient if I use caution, situated on the road near Henin-Lietard.

Everything went as planned and my first thought on landing was "What has become of the other fellow?" He landed a mile from the spot where I had come down.

I had plenty of time to inspect the damage on my plane. It had been hit a number of times. The shot that caused all the damage had gone through both benzene tanks. There was not a drop left and the engine had also been hit. That was a pity for it had worked so well. Minutes later, I was surrounded by a large group of soldiers. Then came an officer, quite out of breath who was very excited. He rushed towards me, gasped for air and asked: "I hope that nothing has happened to you. I have followed the whole fight and am terribly excited! Good Lord, it looked awful!" I assured him that I was quite well, and jumped down and introduced myself. He did not know of my name but offered to take me in his car to Henin-Lietard, where he was quartered.

Driving off, he was still very excited. It suddenly struck him to ask: "Good Lord, but where is your chauffeur?" At first, I didn't understand and probably looked puzzled. Then it dawned on me that he thought I must be the observer of a two-seater plane and he was asking about my pilot. Trying not to laugh, I said: "I always drive myself." The word 'drive' is taboo among flying men. An aviator does not drive; he flies. In the eyes of this kind gentleman I had obviously lost standing once he realised that I 'drove' my own aeroplane and our conversation began to slacken.

Once at his headquarters, he tried to get me to lie down on the sofa, arguing that I was bound to be exhausted after my fight. I assured him that this had not been my first aerial battle. After a while he got round to asking the big question: "Have you ever brought down a plane?" Since he had not recognised my name, I answered nonchalantly: "Oh, yes! I have done so now and then." He replied: "Indeed! Perhaps you have shot down two?" I answered: "No. Not two but twenty-four." He smiled, and repeated his question, adding that he meant not shooting at a plane but hitting it in such a manner that it fell to the ground and remained there. I assured him that I understood the meaning of the words "shooting down."

By now I had lost patience with him. He was convinced that I was a fearful liar and left me sitting where I was, saying that a meal would be served in an hour if I liked to join him. I accepted, slept soundly for an hour and then went to the Officers Club.

I had no uniform under my greasy leather coat, just a waistcoat and apologised for being so badly dressed. Suddenly my host caught sight of my Order de Merit. He was speechless. I gave him my name again, and this time he seemed to recognise it. I fed on oysters and champagne and was looked after gloriously until my orderly arrived in my car to fetch me. Before we left, I assured my kind host that I had now increased my 'bag' to twenty-five.'

Nieuport Scouts of No.1 Squadron RFC seen at Bailleul, France in December 1917. The term 'Scout' in this context covered various models of Nieuport single-seat fighters as witnessed by the various styles of empennage. Von Richthofen accounted for several Nieuport Scouts.

Chapter Six

Defending the Siegfried Line

By early spring 1917, the tide of war was turning on both Eastern and Western Fronts, and German forces were badly stretched. Von Richthofen's squadron was pulled back to defend the Siegfried Line of defensive forts and tank defences constructed as part of the Hindenburg Line along the French border.

'Activity in the air was of course very great. We allowed our enemies to occupy the territory we had evacuated, but we did not allow them to occupy the air as well. The fighter squadron that Boelcke had trained, looked after the English fliers who have transposed a war of position in the air, to a war of movement with the utmost caution.'

My first double event

'2nd April, 1917 was a very warm day. From my quarters I could clearly hear the drumfire of guns, which was again particularly violent. I was still in bed when my orderly rushed into the room shouting: "Sir, the English are here!" Sleepily, I looked out of the window and, yes, there they were circling over the airfield. I jumped out of bed and into my clothes. My 'Red Bird' had been pulled out ready for starting, knowing that I could not allow such a favourable opportunity to go by. I snatched my furs and went.

I was the last to leave. My comrades were much nearer to the enemy and I worried that my prey might escape, leaving me to watch from a distance at the others fighting. Suddenly, one of the impertinent Englishmen tried to drop down on me. I allowed him to come near and then we started a merry dance. My opponent had a two-seater and flew on his back and did other tricks. But very soon I was his master. Victory always goes to the one who is calmest, shoots best and has the clearest brain. After a short time I got him beneath me without hurting him seriously. We were at least a mile from the Front and I thought he intended to land. But suddenly, when only a few metres above the ground, he went off in a straight line, trying to escape. That was too bad. I attacked him again, going so low that I worried I would touch the roofs of houses in the village below. The Englishman defended himself to the end, rushing full speed into a block of houses. This was another case of splendid daring but more foolhardiness than courage, highlighting the difference between energy and idiocy. He paid for his stupidity with his life.

My comrades were still in the air and were very surprised when we met for breakfast that I had scored my 32nd kill. A young Lieutenant had bagged his first plane and we happily prepared everything for further battles.

Later, I was visited by Lieutenant Voss from Boelcke's Squadron who had downed his 23rd plane the previous day and was next to me in the list of kills. When he went to fly home, I offered to accompany him part of the way. We flew in a round-about way over the Fronts, but the weather

Circa 1917: Manfred von Richthofen stroking his pet dog, Moritz. Originally a cavalryman, Richthofen transferred to the Air Service in 1915, becoming one of the first members of *Jasta* 2 in 1916. He quickly distinguished himself as a fighter pilot, and during 1917 became leader of *Jasta* 11 and then the larger unit *Jagdgeschwader* 1 (better known as the 'Flying Circus'). By 1918, he was regarded as a national hero in Germany, and was very well known by the other side. Richthofen was shot down and killed near Amiens on 21 April 1918. There has been considerable discussion and debate regarding aspects of his career, especially the circumstances of his death. He remains perhaps the most widely known fighter pilot of all time, and has been the subject of many books, films and other media.

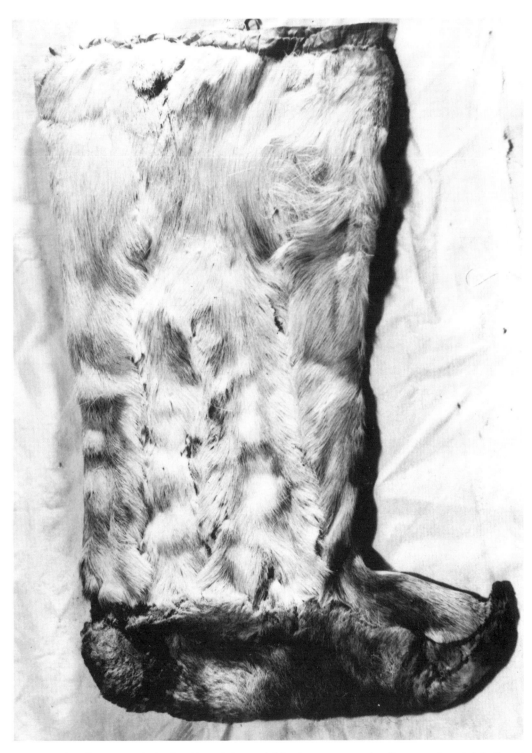

Circa 1918: A First World War fur-skinned thermal flying boot as worn by German pilots. It is believed that this particular example belonged to Baron Manfred von Richthofen.

Manfred von Richthofen is helped into his flying gear; a thick fur-lined coat, cap and fur boots to combat the extreme cold experienced when flying open cockpit aircraft at 10,000ft or more.

Circa 1915: Lieutenant Werner Voss, seated on a motorcycle was a German flying ace credited with 48 aerial victories. He was promoted first to *Gefreiter* on 27 January 1915, and then to *Unteroffizier*, on 18 May 1915 when barely 18 years of age. His service earned him the Iron Cross 2nd Class. He was killed on 23 September 1917.

had turned so bad that we could not hope to find any opponents. Beneath us were dense clouds and Voss, who did not know the country, began to feel uncomfortable. As we passed above Arras, I spotted my brother who is also in my squadron and who had lost his way. Recognising my machine from its colour, he joined us. Suddenly we saw a squadron approaching from the other side and I thought "Now comes number 33." There were nine English planes and although they were over their own territory, they did not venture to fight. We caught them up, and being nearest, I attacked the plane to the rear. To my delight he accepted battle and the pleasure increased when his comrades deserted him. It was to be a single fight just like the one I had had in the morning. My opponent knew what he was about and did not make matters easy for me. He was also a good shot. Then a favourable wind came to my aid, which blew us both over the German lines. He plunged into a cloud and disappeared and might have saved himself. But as luck would have it, after plunging after him, I found myself close behind him when I dropped out of the cloud. We both fired at each other without a tangible result at first, but then I noticed a ribbon of white benzene vapour – I had hit him at last. He would have to land for his engine had stopped.

But he was a stubborn fellow, and though bound to recognize that he had lost the game, continued shooting, defending himself exactly as his fellow countryman had in the morning. He *fought on until forced to land. I flew over him at an altitude of about 30 feet to ascertain whether I had killed him or not. And what did the rascal do? He took his machine-gun and shot holes into my machine! Later, Voss told me if that had happened to him, he would have shot the airman on the ground. I should have done so for he had not surrendered. He was one of the few fortunate fellows to escape with his life. But I was happy and flew home to celebrate my 33rd kill.'*

My record day

April 1917 became known on the Allied side as 'Bloody April' when German airmen pressed home their advantage in aircraft and location. Von Richthofen alone, shot down twenty-one enemy aircraft, which brought his score up to fifty-two, twelve more than Boelcke. He took greatest pride in shooting down four planes in one day.

'The weather was glorious. We were ready to set out when a visitor arrived saying that he had never seen an aerial fight or anything resembling it before. We put him behind a telescope and took off with my friend Schäfer saying that we might give him some fun.

The day began well. We had scarcely reached 6,000 feet when a 5-strong English squadron was spotted coming our way. We attacked in a rush just like a cavalry charge and destroyed the squadron. Three plunged straight into the ground and two went down in flames. None of our men were even wounded.

Circa 1917: The Albatros D.III was used by both the Imperial German Army Air Service (*Luftstreitkräfte*) and the Austro-Hungarian Air Service (*Luftfahrtruppen*) during World War I and was flown by many of the top aces, including von Richthofen, Ernst Udet, Erich Löwenhardt, Kurt Wolff, and Karl Emil Schäfer. It was preeminent during the period of German aerial dominance known as 'Bloody April' in 1917 when it was largely responsible for the Allied losses of 368 aircraft.

A smiling von Richthofen, Commander of *Jasta* 11, surrounded by his fellow pilots who made impressive victory claims during 'Bloody April' in 1917, and his dog Moritz, at Roucourt, France. Left to right: *Vizefeldwebel* Sebastian Festner (nine victories that month, killed on 23 April), Lieutenant Karl-Emil Schäffer (fourteen victories), Manfred von Richthofen (22 victories), his brother *Leutnant* Lothar von Richthofen (14 victories) and *Leutnant* Kurt Wolff (21 victories).

Our visitor below was surprised. He had imagined something quite different and far more dramatic. He thought the whole encounter had looked quite harmless until some planes came falling down like rockets. Gradually I have become accustomed to seeing machines falling down, but the first time I saw an Englishman fall, it really impressed me deeply and I have often relived the event in my dreams.

In the evening we sent off the proud report: "Six German machines have destroyed 13 hostile planes." Boelcke's Squadron had only once made a similar report. Today, the hero was Lieutenant Wolff, a delicate-looking little fellow who nobody would suspect of being a redoubtable champion. He had shot down four of his opponents. My brother had destroyed two, Schäfer two, Festner two and I, three.

One amusing thing occurred. One of the Englishmen we had shot down and was now a prisoner, asked about the red plane. He told us that there was a rumour within his squadron that it was flown by a girl — a kind of Joan of Arc. He was very surprised when I assured him that the supposed girl was standing in front of him. He did not intend to make a joke, but was convinced that only a girl would sit in such an extravagantly painted machine.'

The English attack our airfield

The most suitable nights for flying are when there is a full moon shining. By April 1917 the British were always industrous on such nights, particularly during the Battle of Arras, and not surprisingly, the airfield where Von Richthofen's squadron was based, came in for its share of attention.

'We were in the Officers Mess when the telephone rang: "The English are coming" we were told. There was a great hullabaloo. We dived down into our shelter and at first could hear only a gentle humming, but then came the noise of engines. Their nearest planes were still too far away to be attacked, but we were excited. The only thing we feared was that the English would not find our airfield. To find a spot at night is not easy and our field was particularly difficult because it was not situated near a main road, water or a railway to guide them in. The English circled around at a high altitude and we began to think they were looking for another target. Then, suddenly, the nearest one switched off his engine. He was coming lower.

We had two carbines between us and began shooting. We could not see him but the noise of our gunfire had a sedative effect on our nerves. Then the searchlights picked up the plane half a mile away, flying straight towards us. Everyone started shooting. He came lower and lower, down to about 300 feet, then started his engine and flew straight towards where we were standing. The first bomb fell, followed by a number of others, but the pretty fireworks could only have frightened a coward. Bombing at night has only a moral effect. Those who are easily frightened are strongly affected, but others don't care.

We were greatly amused by the performance of the English and thought that they may come quite often. They dropped their bombs from an altitude of 150 feet, which we thought was rather foolish because if I can hit a wild boar with a rifle at that distance, why should I not succeed in hitting them? Having shot a number of them down from above, it would be a novelty to down an English airman from the ground.

After they had gone, we went back to our mess and discussed how best to receive the English next time they pay us another visit. Over the course of the next day, our orderlies and other fellows worked with great energy to pile foundation posts to mount machine guns in readiness for the following night. These were English machine guns captured from the enemy with their sights rearranged for night shooting. We were curious as to what would happen next.

Sitting in the mess the following night, we were discussing the problem when an orderly rushed in shouting: "They are here! They are here!" before disappearing down the nearest bomb shelter. We rushed to our machine guns. Some of the men known to be good shots were given the machine guns, while the rest were provided with carbines. The whole squadron was armed to the teeth ready to give a warm reception to our visitors. The first plane arrived, just as the previous evening, at a very great altitude before dropping down to 150 feet and got into the glare of the searchlight. When the plane was 300 metres away, someone fired the first shot and the rest joined in. A charge of cavalry or storming troops could not have been met more efficiently than the attack on this single plane flying so low. He would not have heard the noise of our gunfire, over the roar of his engine, but he must have seen the flashes from our guns. I thought it tremendously plucky that he did not swerve, but stuck to his plan and continued flying straight ahead. It would have been silly for flying men to die from a bomb, so just as he flew above us, we jumped into our bomb shelter, and as soon as he had passed over our heads, rushed out again to fire after him. Schäfer, who is quite a good shot, thought he had hit the man, but I did not believe him. Any one of us had just as good a chance at making a hit as he had. But we achieved something, for owing to our shooting, the enemy had dropped their bombs rather aimlessly. One of them, it is true, had exploded only a few metres from my Petit Rouge, but had not damaged it.

We were attacked several times during the night. Once, when I was fast asleep, I dreamed of anti-aircraft firing and woke to discover the reality. One English plane flew so low that I pulled the blanket over my head in fright. The next moment there was an incredible bang, which blew out the window panes in my room. I rushed out to fire a few shots after him and found we were firing from everywhere. This was one opportunity lost.

The next morning, we were delighted to discover that we had shot down no fewer than three Englishmen. They had landed not far from our airfield and were now prisoners of war. The English were less satisfied with the result and from then on, gave our airfield a wide berth. Let us hope that they come back to us next month.'

The anti-Richthofen Squadron

With a fast-growing number of tallies, von Richthofen's distinctive blood-red Fokker became a particular target for the Allied pilots, who became determined to hunt him down. They went so far as to focus one squadron on the task, which only became apparent to the Germans when it became clear that the English pilots were aiming their collective aggression at *La Petit Rouge*. Von Richthofen's men countered this by painting all their planes red.

Spring 1918 Western Front: Fokker triplanes of Richthofen's fighter unit, with Von Richthofen pictured on the right. The Fokker Dr.I Dreidecker (triplane) saw widespread service in the spring of 1918 and became renowned as the aircraft in which Richthofen gained his last 19 victories, and in which he was killed on 21 April 1918.

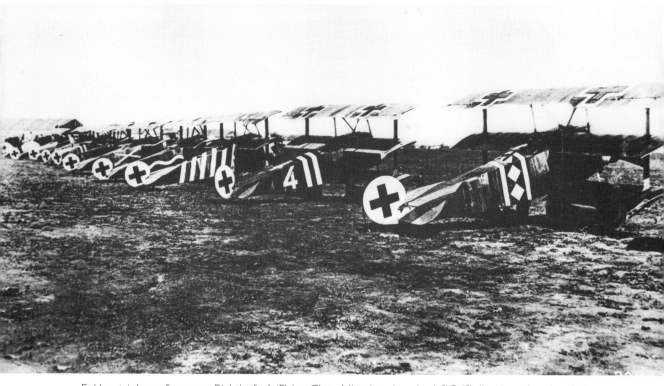

Fokker triplanes from von Richthofen's 'Flying Circus' (*Jagdgeschwader* 1 [JG.1]), lined up showing their variegated appearance. Known as a Flying Circus because all the planes were painted bright colours for easy identification, like a circus, they travelled to wherever they were needed, often by train. Although two pre-production machines had been supplied individually to Richthofen and Voss a little earlier, the Dr.I officially entered service in September 1917 and by spring 1918 was in widespread use – and yet it seems strange to relate, given its iconic status then, and ever since, that the total production of these aircraft amounted to a mere 322 machines. (By comparison, about 5,500 Sopwith Camels and about 5,200 examples of the SE.5a were built) At its peak of service, in April/May 1918, a maximum of perhaps 175 Dr.Is were available on the Western Front. Thereafter its numbers steadily declined, to be replaced by the excellent Fokker D.VII.

'Our new trick did not stop the attacks, and really, I preferred their new tactics for it is better that customers come to one's shop rather than to have to go out and look for them. We flew to the Front hoping to find our enemy and after about 20 minutes, the first arrived and attacked us. Our aggressors were three Spad single-seater planes. Wolff, my brother and I were flying together, so it was three against three, just as it ought to be. I tackled one opponent and could see my brother and Wolff engage the other two. The usual waltzing began as we circled around one another. A favourable wind was blowing away from the front in the direction of Germany. My man was the first to fall. I think I had smashed up his engine. He made up his mind to land but I decided to attack him a second time with the consequence that his whole machine was shot to pieces. Bits of his plane dropped off like pieces of paper and the fuselage fell like a stone, burning fiercely. It dropped into a morass of mud that would have made it impossible to dig it out, so I never

Brothers at arms: Manfred von Richthofen (right) with his younger brother Lothar von Richthofen who served under him in *Jagdgeschwader* 1 (JG.1), standing in front of a Fokker Triplane. Lothar, who was born on 27 September 1894 (died in July 1922), was credited with 40 victories. They were distant cousins of (the later) *Luftwaffe* Field Marshal, Wolfram von Richthofen.

1917: Manfred being helped out of his biplane. Richthofen led his unit to unparalleled success, peaking during 'Bloody April' 1917 when (as related earlier) he downed 22 British aircraft, including four in a single day.

discovered the name of my opponent. He disappeared with only the end of the tail visible marking the place where he had dug his own grave.

Wolff and my brother also forced their opponents to land not far from my victim and we flew home very happy, hopeful that this anti-Richthofen Squadron would return to the fray again.'

A few days later…

'We were flying over the Front with my brother next to me, when I noticed two hostile planes approaching. I waved to my brother who understood my meaning, and we flew side by side, increasing our speed, knowing that we could rely on one another. My brother attacked the first and I took care of the second. I quickly got on the favourable side of my opponent and after a short spell of quick firing, the enemy machine went to pieces. I had never had a more rapid success. While I was following fragments of my enemy's plane, I noticed my brother, scarcely 500 metres away from me, still fighting his opponent. I say that I could not have done any better. He had rushed his man and both were turning around one another. Suddenly, the enemy plane reared up, a sure sign of a hit; probably the pilot had been shot in the head. The machine fell quite close to my victim and we congratulated one another by waving. It is splendid when one can fly with one's brother and do so well.

We were joined by others from our squadron and climbed to a higher altitude to look for the members of the Anti-Richthofen Club. Unfortunately, they were again too high, so we closed formation and waited for their attack. It was our triplanes against their new Spads, but the quality of the plane matters little. Success is dependent on the man sitting in them. The English airmen played a cautious game, refusing to bite. We offered to fight on one side of the Front or on the other, but they appeared to say "No, thank you". What is the good of bringing out a squadron against us and then turning tail? At last, one of their men plucked up courage and dropped down on our rear machine. Naturally, battle was accepted even though our position was an unfavourable one. If you wish to do business you must adapt to the desires of your customers. The Englishman noticed as we all turned round towards him, and got away, but at least battle had commenced.

Another Englishman tried a similar trick on me and I greeted him with quick fire from my two machine guns. He tried to escape by dropping down, which was fatal. Anything in the air that is beneath me is lost, for it cannot shoot to the rear. My opponent had a very fast machine but did not succeed in reaching the English lines. I began firing at him when we were above Lens just to frighten him. He started flying in curves, which enabled me to catch up. I got almost to within touching distance of him, waited until we were 50 metres apart, then took careful aim and fired both the machine guns simultaneously. I heard a slight hissing noise, a certain sign that the benzene tanks had been hit, then saw a bright flame, and he disappeared below. This was my fourth victim of the day. My brother bagged two. We brothers had got six Englishmen in a single day. That is a whole flying squadron. I believe the English will cease to feel any sympathy for us.'

Returning home to a hero's welcome
Von Richthofen celebrated his 50th 'kill' with an invitation to lunch with His Majesty, Kaiser Wilhelm II on 2nd May 1917, his 25th birthday. By then, Manfred had bagged two more victims and was ordered to fly to Cologne, a three-hour flight, to meet the two top-ranked generals, Hindenburg and Ludendorf.

1917: Richthofen (in front) and other Air Service personnel salute during a visit by the Kaiser.

Circa 1917: *General der Infanterie* Erich Ludendorff inspecting *Jagdstaffel* 11 at Marckebeke, Belgium. Von Richthofen's red-painted Albatros D.V, 2059/17, is seen in the background. Ludendorff (9 April 1865 - 20 December 1937), famed for his victory at Tannenberg on the Eastern Front, was appointed Quartermaster General in August 1916, making him joint head with von Hindenburg, as well as chief architect of Germany's war effort until his resignation in October 1918.

An undated image displaying British aircraft serial numbers mounted as trophies on the wall of Richthofen's room at Schweidnitz. At least twelve of the eighteen complete aircraft serial numbers visible were shot down by the Baron himself, ranging from '6580' his fifth kill – a BE.12 in October 1916, to '4997', his forty-third – an FE.2b on 13 April 1917. Note the chandelier, formed from a rotary aero engine possibly salvaged from the wreckage of one of his victims.

Circa 1918: The collection of silver cups and memorabilia collected by Manfred von Richthofen to mark each 'kill'. Each Cup was engraved with the date and type of enemy machine he had shot down. The collection ended at 60 cups because his jeweller in Berlin could not source further silver, and von Richthofen refused to accept cups made from pewter.

'Anthony' Fokker seen (from left to right) with *Leutnant* Krefft, Fokker, Kurt Wolff and Richthofen during a visit to the Fokker aircraft factory at Schwerin in the summer of 1917. *Oberleutnant* Kurt Wolff (February 6 1895 - September 15 1917) was killed in action aged 22 after scoring 33 victories. Anton Herman Gerard Fokker (6 April 1890 - 23 December 1939) was a Dutch aviation pioneer and aircraft manufacturer renown for his fighter aircraft designs produced in Germany during the War.

In addition to the several Albatros biplanes seen on this unidentified airfield, a number of Fokker Dr.Is are apparent, as is a single D.VII, dating this image to 1918, the year in which the D.VII entered operational service.

Richthofen (left) with members of *Jagdstaffel* 5 gathered round another pilot's Fokker Dr.I following Richthofen's 62nd victory (a DH.5) on 23 November 1917.

'It is a weird feeling to be in the room where the fate of the world is decided. I was quite glad to get outside this holiest of holies and go on to lunch with His Majesty. He congratulated me on my success and handed me a small birthday present. I would never have believed it possible that on my 25th birthday I would be sitting to the right of General Field Marshal von Hindenburg and be mentioned in his speech.'

Two days later, Manfred set off again, this time for a spell of home leave. After landing in Nuremberg to refuel, a thunderstorm struck. Being in a hurry to reach Berlin before dark, he took off.

'I enjoyed the clouds and the beastly weather. The rain fell in streams and sometimes it hailed which damaged the propeller so badly the blades looked more like saws. Unfortunately I enjoyed the bad weather so much that I quite forgot to look around me and soon had no idea where I was. What a position to be in! I had lost my way in my own country, and my friends back home will laugh when they find out!

Towns, villages, hills and forests were slipping away below me and I did not recognize a thing. Later I discovered that I was flying about 60 miles off my map. I tried to read the name written on a station, but of course it was too small, and having flown for a couple of hours, my observer and I decided to land. That is always unpleasant, for if one of the wheels lands into a hole, the plane can finish up as matchwood. We looked for a meadow and tried our luck. It was not as pleasant as it looked and we finished up with a slightly bent frame. We had made ourselves look gloriously ridiculous, first by getting lost, and then breaking the machine. We had landed in the neighbourhood of Leipzig and had to make the rest of the journey to Berlin by train.

A few days later I arrived in Schweidnitz, my home town, and though it was only 7 o'clock in the morning, there was a large crowd at the station and it became clear that the people at home took a vivid interest in their fighting soldiers after all.'

In June 1917, The Imperial German Flying Service underwent a major change of strategy, merging *Jagdstaffel* 4, 6, 10 and 11 into one large unit, which became *Jagdgeschwader* 1. Commanded by von Richthofen; it was quickly dubbed 'the Flying Circus'.

While the war was going the Allies way on the ground, Germany had the upper hand in the air until, one day in July, Manfred took a bullet in the head while attacking a squadron of British planes.

'Suddenly, there was a blow to my head. I was hit. For a moment I was completely paralysed. My hands dropped to the side, my legs dangled inside the fuselage. The worst part was that the blow on the head had affected my optic nerve and I was blinded completely. The machine dived down.'

Somehow, von Richthofen regained partial sight and movement at 2,600 feet and managed to land his plane. The wound kept him grounded until mid-August and left him suffering from frequent headaches and depression, but he refused to retire.

Richthofen photographed with a nurse while recuperating from his injuries after receiving a shot to the head during aerial combat in July 1917. He managed to land safely, but it was not until August that he was allowed to fly again.

Manfred was later visited by his father, *Major* Albrecht von Richthofen (1859–1920), while recovering from his head wound.

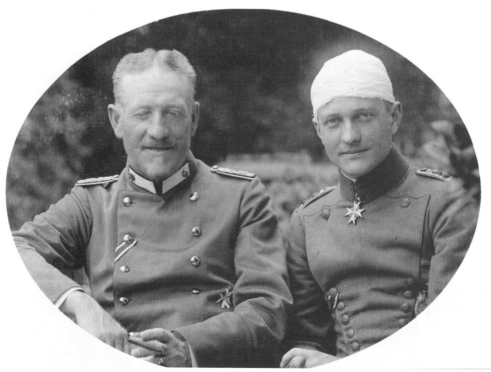

Chapter Seven

The End

Von Richthofen continued to menace Allied aircraft, chalking up eighty confirmed 'kills' before finally succumbing himself. He marked each success by ordering a silver cup engraved with the date and type of enemy machine he had shot down from a jeweller in Berlin, until the dwindling supply of silver in blockaded Germany led to a halt in his collection after 60 cups. He refused to accept cups made from pewter.

His rule to pilots under his command was: 'Aim for the man and don't miss. If you are fighting a two-seater, get the observer first; until you have silenced that gun, don't bother about the pilot.'

His best-known victory against British air ace Major Lanoe Hawker VC, convinced von Richthofen of the need for a fighter aircraft with greater agility, and he went on to champion the development of the Fokker D.VII biplane. He had great influence over the design but never had the opportunity to fly one in combat. Von Richthofen was killed just days before the new plane entered service.

He met his death on 21st April 1918, while flying over Morlancourt Ridge near the River Somme, the day after chalking up his 80th kill. At the time, the German ace was pursuing a Sopwith Camel piloted by novice Canadian pilot Lieutenant Wilfred 'Wop' May of No.209 Squadron, Royal Air Force. The Baron had to break briefly to fend off a high-speed dive attack from another Camel piloted by fellow Canadian Captain Arthur 'Roy' Brown.

Brown was credited with shooting down the Red Baron, but history shows that that it was a ground fire that killed the great flyer. Von Richthofen managed to land his Fokker Dr.I triplane but died moments after men from the Australian Imperial Force (AIR) who controlled the sector, had reached his aircraft. His last recorded word was 'Kaput' – finished.

Number 3 Squadron Australian Flying Corps, assumed responsibility for von Richthofen's remains. In a final ironic twist, the doctor charged with performing an autopsy to determine the cause of death was, as related earlier, Lieutenant Colonel George Walter Barber, a fellow 'old boy' from Whitgift School where Manfred's first victim, 19-year-old Second Lieutenant Lionel Bertram Frank Morris had also gone to school. Barber studied medicine at London University graduating in 1891 before emigrating to Western Australia four years later. He served with the Australian Army Medical Corps throughout the First World War. Barber found that it was not bullets fired from Brown's Sopwith Camel that had 'downed' the Red Baron, but a single .303 bullet that had entered the body travelling upwards through the heart, that killed him – almost certainly fired by Australian forces from the ground.

Von Richthofen's plane was stripped bare by souvenir hunters. As 'Top Gun' on both sides during World War I, he was celebrated in death as much as he had been in life and became a true 20th Century legend.

This image is thought to be the last photo taken of Manfred who is seen on the right with three colleagues. Richthofen was shot down and killed near Amiens on 21 April 1918.

Whereas the Red Baron marked his successes by ordering trophy cups for each of his kills, or at least he did so whilst silver remained available, the cup illustrated here was quite different.

Sent to him by the Emperor himself, its translation is self explanatory and reads …

To the glorious fighter plane pilot Rittmeister Freiherr von Richthofen
Commander of the fighter-squadron number one for his outstanding
achievements in the air-fight
From his grateful emperor and king
Wilhelm
Grand Headquarter, 2nd April 1918

The Sopwith Camel, the type of aircraft which was originally believed to have been responsible for Richthofen's death – since disproved. This British single-seat fighter made its debut on the Western Front in 1917. It featured a short fuselage, a heavy and powerful rotary engine and concentrated firepower courtesy of its twin Vickers' synchronized machine guns. Though difficult to handle the Camel provided unmatched manoeuvrability for experienced pilots. A superlative fighter, the Camel was credited with shooting down 1,294 enemy aircraft – more than any other type of Allied fighter during the First World War. It also served as a ground-attack aircraft, especially near the end of the conflict as it gradually became outclassed in air-to-air combat following the introduction of newer German fighter designs. The Camel was superseded by the Sopwith Snipe.

The remains of Richthofen's triplane. Shot down over Amiens on 21st April 1918, it was later ascertained that a .303 bullet fired from the ground had killed the ace.

The two Spandau machine-guns taken from Richthofen's wrecked plane being examined by officers of No.3 Squadron, Australian Flying Corps at Bertangles on 22 April 1918.

"LE RHONE ENGINE"
Horse Power 110 Makers No 2478.
Ex Capt. Von Richthofen's Machine.
"Fokker Triplane."
Shot down by Capt: Brown. 209. Squad.n

The engine from Richthofen's plane salvaged from the wreckage.

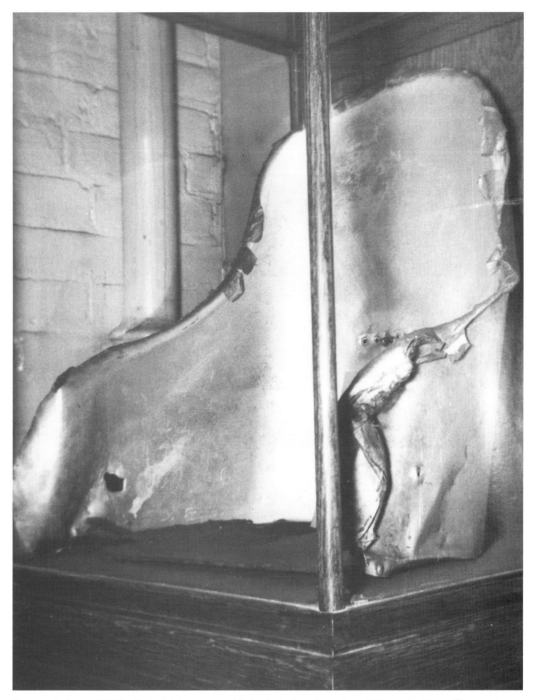

The seat from Richthofen's triplane as exhibited at the Canadian Military Institute. The seat was presented to the Institute by Captain A. Roy Brown, the Canadian pilot credited with shooting Richthofen down over Amiens, France, on 21st April 1918. However, an autopsy report later confirmed that Richthofen had died from a shot fired from the ground, most probably from an Australian contingent fighting on the Allied front line.

The spoils of war. Members of the Australian Flying Corp examine the battered remains of Richthofen's fighter at Poulainville aerodrome in April 1918.

The Funeral of Baron von Richthofen. A firing party from No. 3 Squadron Australian Flying Corps presents arms as the coffin, led by an RAF Chaplan, is carried on the shoulders of six officer pilots. In common with most Allied air officers, Major Blake, who was responsible for Richthofen's remains, regarded the Red Baron with great respect, and organized a full military funeral, to be conducted by the personnel of No. 3 Squadron AFC

The burial of Baron Manfred von Richthofen at Bertangles on 22 April 1918.

The remains of Manfred von Richthofen were removed after World War I and laid to rest in the Invalidenfriedhof Cemetery in Berlin, where many German military heroes and past leaders are buried. The cortege escort was made up of holders of the Pour le Mérite.

The final resting place of Baron Manfred von Richthofen in Berlin. The original flat tombstone was replaced by an upright headstone which was unveiled by the German Air Minister, Hermann Goering in 1937.

Appendix: Heroes of the Air

Top ten air aces from World War I

Victories

1. Rittmeister Manfred von Richthofen (German)	80
2. Capt. René Fonck (French)	75
3. Major E. Mannock (British)	73
4. Lt. Col. William A. Bishop (Canadian)	72
5. Oberleutnant Ernst Udet (German)	62
6. Major Raymond Collishaw (Canadian)	60
7. Capt. James McCudden (British)	57
8 (equal) Capt. Donald MacLaren (Canadian)	54
8. Capt. A. Beauchamp-Proctor (South African)	54
10. (equal) Capt. George Guynemer (French)	53
10. Oberleutnant Erich Löwenhardt (German)	53

1917: Manfred von Richthofen, wearing a leather coat, fur cap and goggles, photographed shortly after landing.

Circa 1918: Major Edward Mannock VC, the leading British ace of the First World War was born in England on 24 May 1887 and subsequently enlisted in the British army prior to applying to join the RFC for pilot training. In early April 1917 Mannock arrived in France and joined No.40 Squadron, gaining his first confirmed aerial victory about one month later. An outstanding exponent of the fighter pilot's craft, Mannock began to increase his score, slowly at first but steadily thereafter. He later became the commander of A Flight No.74 Squadron which was by then equipped with the SE.5a. Following promotion to major in June 1918 he took command of No.85 Squadron RAF (the RFC and RNAS having combined to form the Royal Air Force on 1 April 1918). Mannock was shot down and killed by German ground fire on 26 July 1918, although the award of a VC was not announced in the London Gazette until 18 July 1919.

A further, familiar, image of Major Edward 'Micky' Mannock V.C. D.S.O. Mannock's end was brought about when, in defiance of his own strict ruling, he flew low over the German trenches and was brought down by a fusillade of rifle and machine gun fire. His SE.5a was seen to catch fire before it crashed in German-occupied territory. (Note. In this image, Mannock's uniform displays the rank of captain.)

Oberleutnant Ernst Udet in front of a Fokker D.VII biplane in 1918. Ernst Udet (26 April 1896–17 November 1941) was the second-highest scoring German ace of the First World War and the highest scoring German pilot to survive the war. His 62 victories were second only to the 80 chalked up by his commander, Manfred von Richthofen. Udet rose to become a squadron commander under Richthofen, and later, under Hermann Goering.

1602

Major Ernst Udet seated in a Fokker D.VIII parasol-winged monoplane of which an early example is believed to have flown by April 1918. Although monoplane designs were not unknown in the Great War there weren't many of them, and of those that did fly, several were affected by suspicions governing their structural integrity, a concern that subsequently impacted upon D.VIII production. As a consequence – once the issues had been resolved – only about sixty or so are believed to have entered service by the Armistice. Too late to make any impact on the war, the D.VIII nevertheless offered great agility with an excellent take-off, climb and dive performance.

Captain (as he then was) James McCudden standing in front of Vickers FB.16D, A8963, an experimental fighter with an exceptional top speed – in excess of 135mph at 10,000ft, which could accommodate four forward-firing machine guns (two Lewis and two Vickers). In June 1917 McCudden, then a fighting instructor, flew this plane, and though impressed with its performance, deemed the type unsuitable for service use. Subsequently A8963 was allocated to McCudden as his personal transport until he returned to France in July 1918.

Circa 1918: James Thomas Byford McCudden VC was born on 28 March 1895 descended from a long line of regular army ancestors. In 1910 he joined the Royal Engineers prior to entering the RFC as an Air Mechanic 2nd Class in 1913, and by June 1915 was flying as an observer in two-seat reconnaissance aircraft. His application for pilot training was approved in January 1916, after which, having qualified as a pilot, he joined No.20 Squadron operating the FE.2b and FE.2d in early July 1916. His first aerial victory occurred in early September 1916, by which time he was flying DH.2s with No.29 Squadron. His commission as a second lieutenant became effective from 1 January 1917. Having joined No.56 Squadron in June 1917, McCudden's skill as a fighter pilot increased steadily, as did his score — he accounted for fifty-two of his fifty-seven kills with this unit, his last confirmed kill coming on 26 February 1918. Having left the Squadron in March for a posting to England. the London Gazette announced the award of a Victoria Cross to McCudden on 29 March. Returning to France on 9 July, McCudden took off from Auxi-le-Chateau that evening and was killed when his SE.5a commenced a turn and then rolled over and crashed. McCudden died two hours afterwards.

July 1918: William George 'Billy' Barker VC, DSO & Bar, MC & Two Bars (3 November 1894 - 12 March 1930) was a Canadian fighter ace and Victoria Cross recipient. Major Barker stands in front of his personal Sopwith Camel, B6313, while commanding No.139 Squadron on the Italian Front. Post war, Barker suffered from the physical effects of the wounds he received later in 1918 in which his legs were permanently damaged, and his left arm was left with severely limited movement. He died in 1930 when he lost control of his Fairchild KR-21 biplane trainer during a demonstration flight for the RCAF, at Rockcliffe, near Ottawa, Ontario.

A slightly earlier portrait image of Barker (note the rank insignia on his cuffs). In December 1914, soon after the outbreak of the war Barker enlisted in the 1st Canadian Mounted Rifles. The regiment went to England in June 1915 and then to France on September 22. Barker was a Colt machine gunner with the regiment's machine gun section until late February 1916 when he transferred as a probationary observer to No.9 Squadron RFC flying Royal Aircraft Factory B.E.2 aircraft. After pilot training Barker subsequently flew Camels, gaining his own machine, B6313, while operating in Italy and used it to shoot down several aircraft and balloons over that Front between November 1917 and September 1918. After serving in Italy and a spell as Commander of the fighter flying school at Hounslow Heath, London, Barker returned to France, this time flying the new Sopwith Snipe, he would subsequently be awarded the Victoria Cross following his actions on Sunday, 27 October 1918 while flying the type.

It was while returning his Snipe to an aircraft depot that he crossed enemy lines at 21,000 feet and attacked an enemy Rumpler two-seater, which broke up, its crew escaping by parachute. He was then caught by a formation of Fokker D.VIIs of *Jagdgruppe* 12, consisting of *Jasta* 24 and *Jasta* 44 and found himself in a descending battle against 15 enemy machines. Barker was wounded three times in the legs, then had his left elbow blown away, yet managed to control his Snipe and shoot down three enemy aircraft. The dogfight took place immediately above the lines of the Canadian Corps and he managed to force land inside Allied lines and was transported to a field dressing station. Barker remained in hospital in Rouen until mid-January 1919 when he was transported back to England. He was not fit enough to walk the necessary few paces for the VC investiture at Buckingham Palace until 1 March 1919.

Lieutenant William Leefe Robinson VC, was awarded the Victoria Cross for his aerial attack on a German airship over Cuffley, Hertfordshire – one of 16 that had flown from bases in Germany on a mass raid over England on the night of 2/3 September 1916. Leefe Robinson made an attack at a height of 11,500ft. Approaching from below he closed to within 500ft and raked the wooden-framed Schutte-Lanz airship with gunfire. As he was preparing for another attack, the airship burst into flames and crashed in a field.

Leefe Robinson was later posted to France as a Flight Commander with No.48 Squadron, flying the new Bristol F.2 Fighter. His formation of six aircraft encountered Albatros D.III fighters of *Jasta* 11 led by Manfred von Richthofen, which resulted in four of the British fighters being shot down, including Robinson who was hit by *Vizefeldwebel* Sebastian Festner. Wounded, he was captured and made several attempts to escape, and spent half his imprisonment in solitary confinement which had a detrimental effect on his health. Robinson died on 31 December 1918 and was buried at All Saints' Churchyard Extension in Harrow Weald where a memorial still stands.

Circa 1916: Lieutenant Charles Eugène Jules Marie Nungesser MC, seen leaning on his Nieuport biplane, was a French pilot, ace and adventurer best remembered as a rival of Charles Lindbergh. Nungesser was a renowned fighter pilot, rated third highest in France with 43 credited combat victories by war's end.

Captain Albert Ball VC was a celebrated fighter pilot born in Nottingham. Ball joined the Sherwood Foresters at the outbreak of war and won his commission as a second lieutenant in October 1914. He transferred to the RFC the following year and gained his pilot's wings on 26 January 1916. Joining No.13 Squadron RFC in France, he flew reconnaissance missions before being posted in May to No.11 Squadron, a fighter unit. From then until his return to England, he accrued many aerial victories, earning two Distinguished Service Orders, the Military Cross and Victoria Cross, and was the first ace to become a British popular hero. On 25 February 1917, Ball joined No.56 Squadron and became a Flight commander flying the SE.5 – a type he disliked – and so acquired a Nieuport for his use. On 7 May 1917, Ball, while flying an SE.5 once more, became embroiled in a dogfight with an Albatros D.III and entered a cloud formation from which his aircraft emerged inverted and then crashed behind German lines. His injuries were consistent with the crash only, there being no evidence of any gunshot wounds.

Leutnant Hermann Wilhelm Goering (left) and *Leutnant* Loerzer in front of an Albatros B.II biplane at Stenay. Goering became a fighter pilot during the First World War in which he gained 'ace' status and later became the last commander of *Jagdgeschwader* I, the fighter wing first led by von Richthofen. Goering was awarded the *Pour le Mérite* ('Blue Max') Germany's highest military honour, and after the war, graduated to become politician, military leader and leading member of the Nazi Party. Loerzer learned to fly in 1914 and initially had Goering as his observer until late June 1915. Both men then transferred to fighters. Loerzer flew with *Jagdstaffel* 2 in 1916 before joining *Jagdstaffel* 26 in January 1917. He was credited with 20 victories and received the *Pour le Mérite* in February 1918.

Circa 1914: Major Lanoe George Hawker VC, DSO, was the first pilot to be awarded the Victoria Cross for aerial combat. Born on 30 December 1890, Hawker, a skilled and innovative officer, met his end on 23 November 1916 when he was involved in a dogfight between the DH.2s of No.24 Squadron Royal Flying Corps (RFC) and the pilots of Germany's *Jasta* 2 equipped with the faster Albatros D.II – one of which was flown by Manfred von Richthofen whose score then stood at ten confirmed kills. During the battle Hawker and Richthofen became engaged in a lengthy one-on-one duel over German-held territory, which ended when a single, fatal, round entered Hawker's head and his DH.2 crashed.

Circa 1917: Captain Edward Vernon Rickenbacker, 94th Aero Squadron, American Expeditionary Force. Born in Columbus, Ohio, on 8 October 1890, he became America's leading fighter ace of the First World War with 26 victories, and the recipient of that nation's highest award for valour, the Medal of Honor. Rickenbacker survived the war and died in July 1973.

Circa 1917: Georges Marie Ludovic Jules Guynemer was born in December 1894 to a wealthy and aristocratic family in France. Despite a sickly childhood he nevertheless succeeded as an aviator through his enormous drive and self-confidence. He was originally rejected for military service, but was subsequently accepted for training as a mechanic in late 1914. With determination, he gained acceptance to pilot training and in due course became a fighter pilot who, having mastered the powerful French-manufactured Spad XIII fighter, became a very successful fighter pilot. Guynemer failed to return from a mission near Ypres on 11 September 1917, at which point his number of victories totalled 53, France's leading ace at the time.